PROJECT
PAWsome

OUR TOMORROW

PROJECT PAWSome

Saving Shelter Pets One Bow Tie at a Time

SIR DARIUS BROWN

FOUNDER OF BEAUX & PAWS

Get Creative 6

NEW YORK

GET CREATIVE 6
An imprint of
Mixed Media Resources
19 W. 21st Street, Suite 601
New York, NY 10010

Editor
LAUREN O'NEAL

Creative Director
IRENE LEDWITH

Cover photography
JACK DEUTSCH

Chief Executive Officer
CAROLINE KILMER

President
ART JOINNIDES

Chairman
JAY STEIN

This book is dedicated to all those who have adopted or rescued pets, and to all the PAWsome animal shelters, rescue organizations, and groups that do selfless work caring for homeless dogs and cats until they find FURever homes.

Library of Congress Cataloging-in-Publication Data
Names: Brown, Darius, approximately 2005, author.
Title: Project PAWsome : saving shelter pets one bow tie at a time / Sir
    Darius Brown.
Description: First edition. | New York : Get Creative 6, a Division of Mixed
    Media Resources, [2023] | Series: Our tomorrow | Audience: Ages 8-12
Identifiers: LCCN 2022060954 | ISBN 9781684620708 (paperback)
Subjects: LCSH: Pet adoption--Juvenile literature. | Dog adoption--Juvenile
    literature. | Animal shelters--Juvenile literature. | Animal rescue--Juvenile
    literature.
Classification: LCC SF416.2 .B76 2023 | DDC 636.088/7--dc23/
    eng/20230215
LC record available at https://lccn.loc.gov/2022060954

1 3 5 7 9 10 8 6 4 2

First Edition

Printed in China

Contents

Project PAWsome 7

True Pet Adoption Stories 19

Make a Bow Tie for Pets 86

Animal Shelters 108

Acknowledgments 110

Chapter 1
Project PAWsome

Do you want to make a difference in the world? No matter where you live or how old you are, you can! With a great idea and some hard work, I went from being an ordinary kid to being an award-winning activist and advocate for shelter pets nationwide. Let me tell you my story—and give you tips on how you can make a difference for animals too!

The Teen Behind the Bow Ties

For as long as I can remember, I have loved dogs. Every time I got to play with one, I felt overjoyed. Dogs are so affectionate, intelligent, playful, and loyal. I've always wanted to be a "PAWrent," but my mom was scared of dogs, so I was never allowed to have one of my own. My big sister, Dazhai, and I used to do everything we could to convince our mom to get us a dog, but it never worked. Though I dreamed of going to a shelter and bringing a dog home with me, I never anticipated I would one day become a voice for the voiceless.

"Can I Play with Your Machine?"

Let me give you a little backstory on my life. My sister, Dazhai, is nine years older than I am, and she's my best friend. As a young kid, I was her shadow. I followed her everywhere she went and wanted to do everything she did. When I was seven, Dazhai started a business making wigs and hair bows so she could save up some money for college. I was instantly fascinated with her sewing machine, which I thought was a toy, because it made a loud noise and looked like it would be so fun to play with. I begged Dazhai almost every day to let me play with her "machine," as I called it, but

she didn't let me. At age two, I had been diagnosed with a speech, comprehension, and fine motor skills delay, and although my delays had improved somewhat after many years of therapy, she was still afraid I might hurt myself. Months went by, and I would just sit next to her and watch her use the sewing machine.

Then, one day, when I was eight years old, my therapist told my mom that I should start doing more complex things with my hands to help with my hand dexterity. I tried my luck at asking to help Dazhai again, and just like that, I finally got a yes.

Sir Darius at age 8 with his sister, Dazhai, learning how to sew a bow tie for the first time.

My mother gave me a title; I was now officially Dazhai's assistant. At first, I was only allowed to cut fabric. Cutting fabric taught me how to hold scissors correctly and how to cut a straight line, and it helped with my hand-eye coordination. My role was simple, but boy, was I excited.

As my cutting improved, my mom and Dazhai felt comfortable letting me use the sewing machine for the first time. I was so proud of my first project: a double bow made with Teenage Mutant Ninja Turtle fabric. Dazhai made bows for people to wear in their hair, but as a boy, I didn't want to wear my new creation in my hair.

Sir Darius designing bow ties at age 10.

Dazhai made an elastic neckband for me, I connected it to my bow, and voilà. I was wearing my first handmade bow tie!

I began making and wearing bow ties every chance I could get. Sewing them was fun and relaxing. I enjoyed being creative and mixing different fabrics and colors to come up with attractive designs. I also enjoyed the attention my bow ties got. Whenever I wore them, I would receive compliments from strangers everywhere I went.

One day, a family friend asked me if I could make a custom bow tie for him. I didn't even know what "custom" meant at the time, but I was happy that someone wanted one of my creations. I delivered the bow tie to him personally. Then

Sir Darius sponsors the adoption fee for a pup named Conner at Mt. Pleasant Animal Shelter in New Jersey.

being an animal lover, I started to wonder what was happening to all the animals in the affected areas. Was anyone helping them? I saw a Facebook video about several dogs that were rescued and transported to the New York City ASPCA to be rehomed. I felt relief knowing that the animals were not forgotten and that there were search-and-rescue teams in place to save them, but I still wanted to do my part and help in any way I could.

something happened that I didn't expect: he reached into his pocket and gave me a twenty-dollar bill. It was at that moment I realized that I could follow in my sister's footsteps and start my own business doing something I enjoyed.

Search and Rescue

A few years later, in 2017, Hurricane Harvey made landfall in Texas and Louisiana, causing severe destruction. As I watched it play out on TV from my home in New Jersey, I saw selfless people risking their own lives to save others in need. I was happy to know people were being rescued from the devastation, but,

The New York City ASPCA was not far from where I lived. I felt so bad for those dogs, and I wanted to do something to help them find new homes so they could get out of the shelter and get back to having a family and a normal life. Can you imagine being ripped away from your family, your friends, and your environment, ending up somewhere you don't recognize at all with no idea why? I knew they must be so frightened and confused.

I don't know if it was fate or what, but I immediately thought that if I drew attention and got compliments from people when wearing a bow tie, a dog

would too. That extra attention could help them get adopted faster. I immediately told my mom about my idea. At first, she didn't understand how a bow tie would help, but after I explained it to her, she thought it was a great idea and supported my project 100 percent. I used some of my sister's fabric, and when I ran out, I went to the fabric store to purchase more. In total, I made twenty-five bow ties.

Dazhai accompanied me to the ASPCA, where I met several of the dogs and learned more about shelter pets and their needs. The staff members were impressed with my bow ties and agreed that they would be a great help. They said small accessories like bow ties, bandanas, and necklaces add a little extra swag, which attracts people at adoption events and in photos posted online.

Sadly, I also learned an ugly truth about what happens to dogs and cats in some shelters. Too often, shelters don't have the space to accommodate all the pets they take in, so if the animals don't get adopted or fostered, they're at risk of being euthanized (killed). It broke my

(Top) **Sir Darius with a New York ASPCA staff member.** *(Bottom)* **A pup waiting for a FURever home.**

(Above left) **Sir Darius at Wagmor Pets Dog Rescue in California.** *(Top right)* **Sir Darius at Street Tails Rescue in Philadelphia.** *(Bottom right)* **Sir Darius outside Mt. Pleasant Animal Shelter.**

heart to think that a perfectly healthy dog or cat would lose its life simply due to a lack of space. I thought of how the majority of my immediate family is adopted. There was no expiration date on their lives if they didn't get adopted by a certain time, so why should pets' lives have to end if they weren't adopted?

I thought about this long and hard on my way home from the ASPCA. I was only ten years old, but I made a decision that I would try to save as many dogs' lives as I could by helping them find their forever homes.

From Passion to Purpose

Soon I founded my company Beaux & Paws (pronounced "Bows and Paws"). The concept of Beaux & Paws is simple: for every stylish, handmade bow tie someone purchases from me, I donate an additional bow tie to an animal shelter. Shelters then use the bow ties in photos and at adoption events to make their pets look extra cute and dapper, which helps them get adopted faster. The bow ties come in all different colors and patterns, and they have elastic straps on the back so they can

(Top left) **Sir Darius in front of PAWS Adoption Center in Philadelphia.** *(Bottom left)* **Sir Darius outside BARCS in Baltimore.** *(Above right)* **Sir Darius visits The Barking Lot in California.**

easily slide onto a dog collar.

Beaux & Paws grew quickly, and soon I was donating bow ties to several different local animal shelters. In June of 2019, my story went viral on social media. I began to receive hundreds of requests for bow ties and personal visits to shelters. I was even getting orders and donation requests from people and shelters in other countries!

To help meet their requests, a GoFundMe campaign was created, and I started an initiative called the PAWsome Mission. The goal was to help shelter pets find loving "FURever" homes by donating my bow ties to shelters across the nation, volunteering and participating in adoption events, and spotlighting shelter pets on my social media platforms.

When I announced the PAWsome Mission, so many wonderful people all over the country began to send me fabric, supplies, and donations. Thanks to everyone's incredible generosity, the GoFundMe campaign was a huge success. (In fact, it was so successful that I was named a GoFundMe Kid Hero and was

(Above left) **Sir Darius at Big Apple Circus's first animal adoption event, with its creator and host Jill Rappaport.** *(Above right)* **An adoptable dog from Little Shelter Animal Rescue at the same event.**

interviewed on the company's podcast, *True Stories of Good People*!)

Since starting the PAWsome Mission, I have helped raise over $300,000 to support shelter pets, sponsored adoption fees, donated over 5,000 bow ties to shelters and other organizations, and more. We also make and deliver "Wag Bags" full of pet food, bowls, leashes, and other essential items needed at shelters. So far, I've donated bow ties to at least one shelter in every state (and a few different countries) and visited over twenty-five shelters. I had to pause the initiative in 2020 due to the COVID-19 pandemic, but I used that time to make mittens for the koalas affected by the Australian bushfires and face coverings for essential workers experiencing a mask shortage.

As my impact grew, I started receiving interview requests and even awards. In three years, I did more than 150 interviews! That was great, because I was able to bring more awareness to shelter pets. My work has now been featured in media outlets like CNN, the *Washington Post,* and *Good Morning America*, and I've received awards including the Presidential Volunteer Service Award, the PETA Hero to Animals Award, the Diana Award, and the Global Child Prodigy Award. My proudest moment was when President Barack Obama wrote me a personal letter commending me on my service to the community and on founding Beaux & Paws. It was amazing to realize I wasn't just helping shelter pets, I was also inspiring others around me—including the

BARACK OBAMA

March 8, 2018

Mr. Darius Brown
Newark, New Jersey

Dear Darius:

After hearing your story, I wanted to reach out to commend you for your commitment to community service.

From founding Beaux and Paws to lifting up the lives of those around you, it's clear you are doing your part to look out for your fellow citizens. And I trust you take tremendous pride in all you have accomplished.

As long as you stay engaged in the world around you, continue looking for ways to help others, and never give up on yourself, I'm confident our future will be bright. Know that I'm rooting for you in all you do, and I wish you the very best.

Sincerely,

(Above) **The letter Sir Darius received from President Obama.** (Top right) **Sir Darius, Dazhai, and their mom, Joy, on the** Today **show with Jenna Bush Hager and Heather McMahan.** (Bottom right) **Rachael Ray on set with Sir Darius, Dazhai, and Joy.**

former president of the United States!

I am a young man from Newark, New Jersey, who loves animals and wants to restore people's faith in humanity and in today's youth. I want to inspire and encourage young people everywhere to become change makers. Think about how you can use your talents and skills to help people or animals in need. You don't have to wait until you're an adult. It doesn't matter how old or young you are, what socioeconomic background you come from, what race you are, or what challenges you're faced with. All you need to make a significant difference in the world is a kind heart, creativity, and determination.

You Can Help Animals Too!

Do you love to be around dogs and cats? Do you want to make an impact in your community? Animal shelters rely on volunteers to thrive! Volunteering at a shelter doesn't just help the animals—it's a rewarding opportunity for you as well. Not only are you giving your time and energy to a great cause, you're also gaining a wealth of knowledge and experience you can use as a pet owner or even in a future animal-related career like veterinary medicine. You'll make new friends (animal and human), develop responsibility and time-management skills, and log community service hours. Volunteering is also beneficial for your physical, emotional, and mental health.

What do you need in order to volunteer at an animal shelter? Every shelter has different requirements, but here are some of the most common ones:

- Be the minimum age required by the shelter (usually around eight).
- Have permission from (or be accompanied by) a parent or guardian.
- Submit an application with references.
- Attend orientation and training.

Animal shelters are generally pretty flexible, so you can usually volunteer at times when you're free, such as on the weekends, during holidays, and over summer break.

I'm going to be honest: volunteering

Sir Darius during a visit to Mt. Pleasant Animal Shelter.

at an animal shelter can be emotional sometimes. You may bond with a pet that gets adopted, and although you're happy they found a forever home, you'll miss them greatly. You may form an attachment with a sick or unwanted pet that will never be adopted, and that's hard to watch in a different way. And realizing you can't take all the animals home with you is always a bit of a heartbreak as well. You have to remember why you're there: to support the animals and the shelters. It's all worth it in the end when you remember the difference you're making in these animals' lives.

What Volunteers Do

What kinds of things will you do if you volunteer at a shelter? Duties often include the following:

- Walk and play with the dogs and cats
- Bathe and groom the dogs and cats
- Clean the kennels
- Fill water and food bowls
- Restock supplies
- Take photos of adoptable pets
- Help out at adoption events
- Help raise money
- Foster a pet

How to Contact Your Local Shelter

Ready to volunteer? Contact your local animal shelter to find out how you can help. Start by typing "animal shelter" and your city's name into Google. Once you find a local shelter's website, look for their contact information. (If they have a page labeled "Volunteer," that's a great place to start!) You can then call, email, or visit in person and ask how you can volunteer. Be ready to fill out an application and provide references if necessary!

Other Ways to Help

Not everyone can volunteer at a shelter, but don't worry—there are plenty of other ways you can help. Here are the top four.

1. Adopt your pet from a shelter.
Instead of buying from a pet store, adopt your dog or cat from a rescue or shelter. This saves the lives of two animals: the one you adopt and the next animal who takes their place at the shelter. If you have your heart set on a specific breed (like a golden retriever or corgi) that your local shelter doesn't have, find a rescue organization for that breed rather than a breeder, or use a site like Petfinder.com.

2. Spay or neuter your pet. Dogs and cats can have as many as twelve babies at a time! If an owner can't find homes for all those babies, they will end up in shelters, where they may be euthanized. Spaying (for females) or neutering (for males) is a surgery that prevents your pet from having babies, which helps solve the problem of overcrowded shelters.

3. Get your pet microchipped. If a lost pet doesn't have a microchip or collar, it can be extremely difficult to find that pet's owner. Not only is this stressful for both the pet and the owner, it also means the pet could be taking up space in a shelter and may even be euthanized. Microchip your pet to make sure you can be reunited quickly and happily!

4. Donate to your local shelter. From pet food to cleaning supplies to vet bills, animal shelters have a lot of costs. If you can't donate time, consider donating money, food, and/or supplies instead—and spread the word to others to do the same.

Chapter 2

True Pet Adoption Stories

There's no better feeling than knowing a shelter pet is safe and happy with a loving adopted family. In this chapter, I'm proud to bring you the stories of some of those animals and how they found their FURever homes. Their tales (and adorable photos!) will melt your heart and make you smile.

NAME: CEDRIC GEORGE
OWNER: KARIN
BREED: PUG
AGE: 9
ADOPTED FROM: ROAD DOGS
DISLIKES: DOORBELLS, GOING TO THE VET
LIKES: WATERMELON, BANANAS, RUBBER BALLS, STROLLER RIDES

What was your dog's life like before being rescued?

Cedric was one of a large group of pugs and French bulldogs that a breeder couldn't sell, so they were going to be killed. They were rescued and brought to Road Dogs in the Los Angeles area.

What happened when you saw or met your dog for the first time?

Just a month before I picked Cedric up, I had to say goodbye to my fifteen-year-old rescue pug, Dexter. I wasn't emotionally ready to adopt, but I agreed to foster. My friend and I went down to the airport on a Friday night to wait for the pugs and Frenchies to get off the plane. When they handed me Cedric, I just wanted to erase all his bad memories of his former life.

How did you know this was the dog for you?

After a week of fostering Cedric, I knew he was going to stay forever. My rescue Frenchie showed him the ways of being a spoiled dog, and all the neighbors fell in love with him. He was so curious and excited about everything—walks, car rides, treats, even getting a bath. After five days of sleeping in his crate, he insisted on sleeping in the bed with me, and that's when I knew he was staying forever!

How would you describe your dog's personality?

He's definitely a mama's boy! Cedric is obsessed with getting treats and loves taking stroller rides around town. The minute I grab the water bottle, he knows we're off for an adventure. He has warmed up to all the neighbor dogs, and he loves to go to Grandma and Grandpa's house. He has gained so much confidence since I adopted him.

How has your life changed since adopting your dog?

I wasn't ready for another pug when I lost my Dexter, but Cedric made me realize I still have so much love in my heart for another pup. I know that I have loved his horrible past away. I am so honored I get to take care of him.

How has your dog's life changed since being adopted?

It's night and day! He wakes up excited to see what the day brings. He no longer fears anything and trusts me so much.

How has Sir Darius's work impacted or inspired you?

I used to work at *Access Hollywood* and we had Sir Darius on as a guest. I started following him on social media because I was so inspired by his passion and love for rescue dogs and getting them into good homes!

NAME: WARWICK
OWNER: CHRISTINE
BREED: GOLDEN RETRIEVER
AGE: 2
ADOPTED FROM: PAWS RESCUE QATAR
DISLIKES: STAYING HOME ALONE
LIKES: CHICKEN, CHEESE, WALKS

What was your dog's life like before being rescued?

Warwick was dumped on a goat farm in Qatar as a baby. People from his rescue found him there and took him in. He was covered in ticks and fleas. He had tick fever and had been surviving on goat milk. He was fostered in Qatar until he was nine months old and then was brought to New York City.

What happened when you saw or met your dog for the first time?

Warwick was so friendly and outgoing from the start! He was sweet and trusting, which was amazing, given all he went through to get here. We knew at once he was a very special dog.

How did you know this was the dog for you?

His eyes were so kind and gentle.

How would you describe your dog's personality?

Funny, loving, smart, goofy, sensitive.

How has your life changed since adopting your dog?

Warwick is a member of our family, and our lives revolve around him in many ways. We realized quickly he was too special to keep to ourselves and had him certified as a therapy dog. We visit a hospital once a week and are involved with a school program where we serve at-risk schoolchildren in New York. This has allowed us to give back to the community and make a difference in so many lives.

How has your dog's life changed since being adopted?

Warwick has become more confident. He knows he is in his forever home and is so much calmer as a result.

How has Sir Darius's work impacted or inspired you?

We were inspired by Sir Darius's work and just had to purchase a bow tie for Warwick to support the cause! So many shelter dogs deserve a good home, and we are grateful he's helping to make that happen.

An adorable dog getting ready for transport at Houston PetSet.

SHELTER NAME: HOUSTON PETSET
LOCATION: HOUSTON, TEXAS

YEAR FOUNDED: 2004

MISSION STATEMENT: Our mission is to end the homelessness and suffering of companion animals and elevate their status in society.

How many pets have you found homes for?

We have transported thousands of animals out of Houston shelters since beginning our transport program in 2017.

Why should people adopt shelter dogs instead of purchasing dogs from stores or breeders?

Most animals who wind up in shelters are not there because something is wrong with them, but rather because their owners couldn't give them the life they deserved. Adopting a pet means they get another shot at a happy life filled with love!

What do you love about this line of work?

Helping people is as important as helping animals. Houston PetSet is proud of our work to keep animals with the families that love them in addition to working toward an end to animal homelessness.

How did you start working with Sir Darius?

We ordered a batch of bow ties to send with some of our transported pets for Valentine's Day in 2022. We felt the bow ties would help draw attention to these long-term shelter pets and give them an extra boost for adoption. The bow ties certainly attract the attention of potential adopters and make the pets look extra dapper!

How has Sir Darius's work impacted or inspired you?

We admire and appreciate all of the incredible initiatives Sir Darius has started. It is so encouraging to see the youth of today working toward a better life for animals tomorrow. Houston PetSet is grateful for the opportunity to work together with an inspiring gentleman like Sir Darius, and we look forward to ending the homeless-animal crisis with his help!

NAME: **BEAU**

OWNER: **DAZHAI (SIR DARIUS'S SISTER AND COFOUNDER OF BEAUX & PAWS)**

BREED: **PITBULL**

AGE: **2**

ADOPTED FROM: **HUMANE RESCUE ALLIANCE DC**

DISLIKES: **CLEANING APPLIANCES, BATH TIME**

LIKES: **TREATS, TOYS, SALMON, ZOOMIES, WALKS, AND CUDDLES**

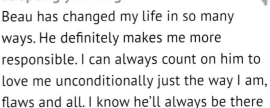

What was your dog's life like before being rescued?

Beau was abandoned for six months before I adopted him. He had lived in a house with a cat, and the previous owner brought him back to the shelter because the two pets could not get along.

What happened when you saw or met your dog for the first time?

When I first met Beau, the animal shelter informed me that he is a staff favorite and a very calm dog. To my surprise, he also had a hidden talent: he can jump very high! Immediately I was drawn to his energetic yet relaxed personality.

How did you know this was the dog for you?

There's a saying: You don't choose a dog, the dog chooses you. Beau is a very quiet dog—I probably hear him bark twice a month. But when I saw him in the kennel, he gave me the loudest bark and the highest jump! I knew he was mine at that moment.

How would you describe your dog's personality?

My fur-baby is full of surprises. You truly don't know what you will get with him. One moment he's lying down wanting cuddles, the next he's jumping off the couch and activating full zoomie mode.

How has your life changed since adopting your dog?

Beau has changed my life in so many ways. He definitely makes me more responsible. I can always count on him to love me unconditionally just the way I am, flaws and all. I know he'll always be there (especially if I have a piece of salmon).

How has your dog's life changed since being adopted?

When I first adopted Beau, he was frail, skinny, and scared. I nurtured him to health, and soon enough he was smiling, belly up, waiting for his belly rubs.

How has Sir Darius's work impacted or inspired you?

As Sir Darius's older sister, I was able to share my love of animals with him growing up, even though our mom was afraid of animals. We always lived in apartments that didn't allow dogs, so the moment I was old enough to live on my own, I went to my local shelter and found the fur-baby I always wanted! There are countless shelter pets in need of homes and love. The volunteers do everything they can to provide what the pets need, but in the end, they need to be adopted into a stable environment.

Fred, a volunteer pilot and host of *The Fred Show*, poses with a Pilots N Paws pup.

SHELTER NAME: PILOTS N PAWS

LOCATION: MORE THAN 6,000 PILOTS LOCATED IN ALL 50 STATES

YEAR FOUNDED: 2008

MISSION STATEMENT: Pilots N Paws is a charitable organization that connects people who rescue, shelter, and foster animals with pilots and plane owners who volunteer to fly these animals where they need to go free of charge.

How many pets have you found homes for?

More than 220,000 animals have been flown through Pilots N Paws. Not only dogs but also cats, service animals, and injured wildlife, including deer, bears, dolphins, eagles, and sea turtles.

How do you ensure the pets go to a good home?

The rescues work with the adopters to assess that the new home will be a great fit for the shelter pet. The pilots are also very adept at assessing situations, and quite often they stay in touch with the people they fly the pets for, receiving holiday cards and regular updates. We get emails on a regular basis sharing beautiful updates of how loved and happy the pets are in their new homes!

Why should people adopt shelter pets instead of purchasing pets from stores or breeders?

We emphasize the mantra "Adopt, don't shop." There are a lot of incredible animals that need loving homes in the shelters. If you need or prefer certain breeds, purebred animals can often be found in shelters. Millions of very adoptable animals are euthanized each year, and Pilots N Paws is helping to change that by widening the field of where adoptions can take place and flying the animals to new homes.

What do you love about this line of work?

We love seeing animals that likely never would have been adopted locally in the loving arms of their new families after they've been flown to an area where a forever home exists!

How did you start working with Sir Darius?

Fred, one of our volunteer pilots, hosts the morning radio show *The Fred Show*. Fred connected with Sir Darius, and the rest is history!

What impact have Sir Darius's bow ties made on your adoptions?

Often, potential adopters find rescue pets online by viewing photographs, and Sir Darius's bow ties add some fun and glamour to attract more attention to the pictures. These animals are all unique and special, just like Sir Darius's bow ties!

How has Sir Darius's work impacted or inspired you?

We've had the pleasure of knowing Sir Darius for years, and have watched him and his mission grow from something small to a national brand! His thoughtfulness, caring spirit, and exuberance are apparent in everything he does, and his passion for animals and their welfare is infectious.

NAME: **ASCHER**
OWNER: **JULIE**
BREED: **YORKSHIRE TERRIER**
AGE: **14**
DISLIKES: **SNOWPLOWS**
LIKES: **CUDDLES, FOOD, PUZZLES, WEARING BOW TIES**

What was your dog's life like before being rescued?
He had behavioral issues and needed a home. He was almost one year old.

What happened when you saw or met your dog for the first time?
He was scraggly looking. I had recently lost a previous Yorkie and was terrified of loving again.

How did you know this was the dog for you?
He had emotional baggage. (Kinda like me!)

How would you describe your dog's personality?
He's very loving. Ascher is my furry soulmate.

How has your life changed since adopting your dog?
He saved my life! I was diagnosed with cancer. Shortly after, so was Ascher. We're getting through this battle together.

How has your dog's life changed since being adopted?
He's not scared of everything anymore!

Patriotic Pups

In January of 2021, the nation celebrated the inauguration of President Joe Biden and First Lady Jill Biden. Pet lovers across the United States also celebrated the "indoguration" of Major Biden, the first-ever rescue pup to become First Dog, having been adopted from the Delaware Humane Association several years prior. The virtual event was attended by close to 10,000 people and raised more than $200,000 to help shelter pets like Major find loving FURever homes.

The highlight of the event was the announcement of the patriotic pup who would serve as Secretary of Rescue Dogs. I had the honor of choosing the winner and creating custom bow ties for all five finalists. I also created an exclusive bow tie to be purchased by PAWrents of pups who attended, with the proceeds benefiting the Delaware Humane Association.

Chosen from among more than 750 applicants, the finalists included Dash, a dog who contributes to science by participating in a canine cognition lab; Billy, a therapy dog who comforts families and hospital patients in Philadelphia; Jonathan, a dog who survived living with his siblings alone in the woods and whose owner sells

Harper is named Secretary of Rescue Dogs.

artwork to raise money for shelters; and Nora, a dog rescued from Iraq who works with veterans with PTSD.

The pup I ultimately selected as Secretary of Rescue Dogs? Harper, who visits nursing homes as a therapy dog and helps kids improve their reading skills with the Paws 2 Read program. Dogs like Harper help make America PAWsome!

NAME: THAI
OWNER: JASSMINE
BREED: SHIBA INU MIX
AGE: 11
ADOPTED FROM: SOUTHERN OREGON HUMANE SOCIETY
DISLIKES: THUNDER, FIREWORKS
LIKES: CHICKEN, BASKING IN THE SUN, TAKING LONG WALKS AND THEN LONGER NAPS

What was your dog's life like before being rescued?

Thai was a street dog in Thailand before being rescued. We don't know much about his life before us, but we do know he had a very rough start, so we're trying to make up for it now with lots of love!

What happened when you saw or met your dog for the first time?

I knew Thai was a perfect fit for our family the first time I met him. He was one of the only dogs that came to the kennel door when I walked up, and it broke my heart to leave without him. Although he was rather aloof when I came back with my husband, we were both sure that he would come out of his shell once we earned his trust.

How did you know this was the dog for you?

After I met Thai, I couldn't stop thinking about having him as part of our family! I knew he had a difficult start to life and that he just needed someone with patience to earn his trust.

How would you describe your dog's personality?

Thai is a jack of all trades! He has no shortage of stubbornness and independence from his Shiba side, but he is also one of the most affectionate, gentle, loving dogs you'll ever meet. He tells you exactly what he wants, when he wants it, whether it be belly rubs, a walk, or bedtime. He never fails to make us laugh or melt our hearts with his unique personality.

How has your life changed since adopting your dog?

Our lives have changed entirely! Thai is the center of our world, and I can't imagine a moment without him. We've worked through separation anxiety and trust issues together, battled some health issues from his past on the street, and shared some of the most amazing experiences together. He truly is an irreplaceable best friend, and I wouldn't trade him for the world.

How has your dog's life changed since being adopted?

When Thai first joined our family, he suffered severe separation anxiety and was very fearful of men. He got carsick easily and couldn't go within a mile of another dog. Today, Thai has overcome his anxiety and has learned to trust people of all shapes and sizes. Car rides are one of his favorite things (he hasn't gotten sick in years), and you can catch him with his head out the window taking in the world. He's learned to play with other dogs, welcomes any and all belly rubs, and spends at least eighteen hours per day sleeping in one of his four beds.

One of the many lovely adoptable dogs at Nashville Humane Association.

SHELTER NAME: NASHVILLE HUMANE ASSOCIATION

LOCATION: NASHVILLE, TENNESSEE

YEAR FOUNDED: 1946

MISSION STATEMENT: Nashville Humane is committed to promoting humane education, controlling pet overpopulation, and finding responsible homes for the homeless and adoptable pet community in Nashville and throughout Tennessee. NHA has been voted "Best Shelter" and "Favorite Not-For-Profit" year over year, and is proud to have a save rate of 99 percent.

How many pets have you found homes for?

We find homes for approximately 3,500 animals a year.

How do you ensure the pets go to a good home?

It is really important to us that our pets find a permanent home! Therefore, adoption applicants must meet adoption requirements before taking their new furry friend home. Interested adopters can visit with our wonderful cats and dogs, and NHA pet service representatives are available to provide advice on selecting the best match for the adopter. They will schedule a meet and greet between family members (including those with four legs) and the prospective pet, to help determine which animal is the best match for the adopter's lifestyle.

Why should people adopt shelter pets instead of purchasing pets from stores or breeders?

Every shelter seems to be overflowing with hopeful, wonderful, adoptable animals worthy of love and a family. Adopting saves the life of that animal and also the next one to take its place in the shelter.

What do you love about this line of work?

There's so much to love! We love welcoming all the animals and assuring them that they're in a safe and loving place. It's also incredible to see a dog overcome their fears and gain their trust. To be a part of that journey is so special. And there's nothing like seeing the face of an adopter when we bring out their pet once the adoption process is over.

What impact have Sir Darius's bow ties made on your adoptions?

The bow ties are eye-catching and look great in pictures!

How has Sir Darius's work impacted or inspired you?

We are so impressed and appreciative of Sir Darius's passion to help shelter pets! He is so kind and thoughtful. It's amazing to see someone so young with an abundance of compassion. We are humbled and honored to be a friend of Sir Darius's, and we know that he will continue to do great things. We are grateful to be a part of his journey!

NAME: LEELOO
OWNER: CAITLIN
BREED: PIT BULL/TERRIER MIX
AGE: 1
ADOPTED FROM: NASHVILLE HUMANE ASSOCIATION
DISLIKES: BATHS, RAIN, RACCOONS
LIKES: CUDDLING, TREATS, KIDS, SWIMMING IN THE RIVER, TEARING APART TOYS IN RECORD TIME

What was your dog's life like before being rescued?

I was told she had been in and out of the shelter twice before, not because of anything she did but because the adopters didn't have the capacity or ability to care for her. Other than that, I don't know anything about her history.

What happened when you saw or met your dog for the first time?

She ran right over, gently jumped up, then kind of collapsed against me and let me scratch her ears and pet her. Then she did the same to my dad, who had accompanied me to the shelter. She seemed less enthused about being outside than about being in our company.

How did you know this was the dog for you?

I can't really explain it. It just felt right. Part of it was definitely how attentive and affectionate she was—those were traits I really wanted in a dog—but when it came down to the question "Do I take her home?," the answer was just "Yes!"

How would you describe your dog's personality?

She is a sweet and intuitive cuddle bug.

How has your life changed since adopting your dog?

I laugh more on a daily basis. I feel healthier both mentally and physically. We take at least two long walks a day, and within two weeks I started seeing wildlife I'd never seen before and found trails and parks I'd never explored. She gets me out to enjoy the sunshine and keeps me company cuddled up inside when it's raining.

How has your dog's life changed since being adopted?

I wish I could ask her that! I definitely think it has changed for the better. I'd guess she has more treats to eat and more comfy places to sleep.

How has Sir Darius's work impacted or inspired you?

I am so touched by his work and his compassion. Thank you, Sir Darius!

NAME: PEANUT
OWNER: HOPE
BREED: LAB MIX
AGE: 1
ADOPTED FROM: NASHVILLE HUMANE ASSOCIATION
DISLIKES: PEOPLE WAITING BY OUR HOUSE
LIKES: ROPE TOYS

What was your dog's life like before being rescued?
We don't know much—she was found on the street.

What happened when you saw or met your dog for the first time?
Joy. She was so sweet and happy.

How did you know this was the dog for you?
She had a great energy about her and was very friendly.

How would you describe your dog's personality?
Sweet and loving.

How has your life changed since adopting your dog?
She has brought a lot of joy into our lives. Our beloved Chihuahua, Pico, passed away recently, and we had been very sad. Adopting Peanut has brought a lot of happiness back to our lives.

How has your dog's life changed since being adopted?
She and my other rescue dog are happy to have each other as companions.

How has Sir Darius's work impacted or inspired you?
Peanut was wearing one of his bow ties at the shelter, which made her look extra adorable!

NAME: ASHLEY

OWNER: PAM

BREED:
GERMAN SHEPHERD/PIT BULL MIX

AGE: 10

ADOPTED FROM:
HAYWARD ANIMAL SHELTER

DISLIKES: OTHER DOGS

LIKES: "FIND IT" GAMES,
NOSEWORK, WALKS

What was your dog's life like before being rescued?
She came into the shelter full of scars. She may have been used in dogfighting.

What happened when you saw or met your dog for the first time?
I was a volunteer at Hayward Animal Shelter when she came in, and she picked me pretty quickly. Any time I took her to the play yard, she just wanted to sit with me. I already had another rescue at home and had no intention of having two dogs. Well, I've had her for eight years now.

How did you know this was the dog for you?
She picked me. She didn't give me much of a choice, and I'm glad.

How would you describe your dog's personality?
Sweet, intelligent, loves to work. She's not much for snuggling, and attention is on her terms. She's loaded with personality, which I love.

How has your dog's life changed since being adopted?
She came into the shelter very thin and abused. Now she is my princess.

How has Sir Darius's work impacted or inspired you?
I am a longtime volunteer at Oakland Animal Services, and dog rescue is my passion. I applaud Sir Darius's actions, bringing dog rescue to the forefront.

A puppy from Jersey Shore Animal Center headed to his FURever home.

SHELTER NAME: JERSEY SHORE ANIMAL CENTER

LOCATION: BRICK, NEW JERSEY

YEAR FOUNDED: 1981

MISSION STATEMENT: The mission of the Jersey Shore Animal Center is to rescue, care for, and rehome unwanted, abused, abandoned, and sick animals. Our goal is to adopt these special animals to the caring and loving forever homes they so richly deserve.

How many pets have you found homes for?

We don't know the exact number because our computerized database doesn't go back forty-one years, but we've found homes for thousands of animals.

How do you ensure the pets go to a good home?

All applicants are screened with a thorough written application, vet references, and physical meet and greets of all family members (including other pets).

Why should people adopt shelter pets instead of purchasing pets from stores or breeders?

There are too many homeless shelter pets, and many will not make it out of shelters due to overcrowding. It starts with education and helping to prevent overpopulation. Spay or neuter your pets!

What do you love about this line of work?

There is nothing more rewarding than helping innocent and defenseless animals who have no control over their situation. Our motto since our fortieth anniversary last year is "Forty Years of Changing Lives"! We're changing the lives of both the pets and the humans who love them.

How did you start working with Sir Darius?

We became aware of Sir Darius through social media and news articles when he first started making the bow ties and visiting shelters. And thankfully we were on his radar!

What impact have Sir Darius's bow ties made on your adoptions?

One of the most important times for our team is when the animals get to meet potential adopters, and hopefully the meetings turn into "gotcha days" (days when people adopt an animal). Sir Darius's bow ties are a wonderful way to bring attention to the animals, especially the ones that are typically overlooked because they're shy or nervous.

How has Sir Darius's work impacted or inspired you?

Knowing that Sir Darius started at such a young age makes it even more amazing and heartwarming to witness his passion and unwavering love for animals. He has such a huge heart and sets such an example of being a role model and paying it forward.

NAME: KATO
OWNER: BJ
BREED: GERMAN SHEPHERD
AGE: 1
ADOPTED FROM: JERSEY SHORE ANIMAL CENTER
DISLIKES: NONE
LIKES: TENNIS BALLS

What was your dog's life like before being rescued?

He was found on the streets of Shelbyville, Tennessee, went to a loving foster home for three weeks, and then was transported to the Jersey Shore Animal Center, where he received lots of love and training.

What happened when you saw or met your dog for the first time?

I will never forget the day I met my main man, Kato! He came into the room, blew past the trainer, came right up to me, put his front paws on my lap, and started licking my face with lots of love. That was a special moment, when I knew this was the "chosen one"!

How did you know this was the dog for you?

His affectionate greeting made me feel assured this was the one, but the real test was the walk. I knew I had to prove I could handle him on a walk. I have lots of experience walking two German shepherds at a time, so I was confident it would go smoothly, and it did. Kato responded to my commands very well and connected with me strongly and immediately.

How would you describe your dog's personality?

Kato is very loving. He is eager to please and looks forward to meeting people. He is very caring with kids and has a special gift when it comes to kids with special needs. He almost seems telepathic.

How has your life changed since adopting your dog?

I had previously had two German shepherds, but both had recently passed away—the two worst days of my life. There was a hole in my heart. Kato has filled that void. My house is a home again.

How has your dog's life changed since being adopted?

Kato is with me almost all day. He goes on errands with me and even comes to work with me—I own a martial arts dojo. Kato is my sidekick! He helps me inspire and train students of all ages, especially kids and especially those with special needs. He's so good with helping others that I'm looking into getting him certified as a therapy dog or search-and-rescue dog.

How has Sir Darius's work impacted or inspired you?

When I took Kato home, he was wearing one of Sir Darius's handsome bow ties!

NAME: REBEL
OWNER: JENNIFER
BREED: LAB/HOUND MIX
AGE: 9 MONTHS
ADOPTED FROM: JERSEY SHORE ANIMAL CENTER
DISLIKES: VACUUMS, BEING LEFT ALONE
LIKES: CHEWING ON ANYTHING, PLAYING WITH HIS SISTER LUCILLE

What happened when you saw or met your dog for the first time?

Our three boys instantly fell in love with Rebel and wanted to bring him home so he could be part of our family. He and Lucille, our hound mix, splashed around in a kiddie pool during the meet and greet.

How did you know this was the dog for you?

We'd lost our dog Negan to lymphoma a few months earlier and wanted another dog, but it was important that Lucille felt comfortable with the new addition. When Lucille gave Rebel the thumbs-up, we knew he was the one.

How would you describe your dog's personality?

As a young, high-energy dog, Rebel is constantly on the go. He is very sweet and likes to give hugs and kisses. He can be a little timid in new environments, so having a big sister to show him the way gives him confidence.

How has your life changed since adopting your dog?

Life with three boys and two dogs is a little more hectic, but he fits into our family very well. He and Lucille love to go on walks together and explore.

How has your dog's life changed since being adopted?

Rebel has three boys who play with him and a big canine sister to lean on. He has lots of new toys to chew on...and some new cat siblings that he's still not sure about.

How has Sir Darius's work impacted or inspired you?

Rebel was wearing a bow tie on the day that we adopted him, and he looked very stylish in it.

NAME: JAXON
OWNER: NICOLE
BREED: BOXER MIX
AGE: 5
ADOPTED FROM: NORTH SHORE ANIMAL LEAGUE
DISLIKES: NONE
LIKES: BALLS, TREATS, THE DOG PARK, CAR RIDES

What happened when you saw or met your dog for the first time?

When I first saw Jax, I knew he would be mine! He was the cutest little pup!

How did you know this was the dog for you?

When I went up to him on the adoption bus, I knew Jax would be a good fit. He had such a lovely personality and was such a sweetheart!

How would you describe your dog's personality?

Jax is silly, smart, and very loving.

How has your life changed since adopting your dog?

Jax coming into my life has made me happier. He was the missing piece to my family, and now it's complete! He makes me laugh all the time with his personality.

How has your dog's life changed since being adopted?

Jax gets so much love! He plays at the dog park and with his sister Rosie. He always gets so much attention from friends and family.

How has Sir Darius's work impacted or inspired you?

Sir Darius got to meet Jax before I did, on the *Rachael Ray Show*, where he had Jax in one of his bow ties! I then went to an adoption event for North Shore Animal League, where I met Jax. Sir Darius does an amazing job!

Maggie, a Southeast Asian village dog from Thailand fostered by Barking Lot volunteer Chelsea (@theserialfoster).

SHELTER NAME: THE BARKING LOT

LOCATION: SAN DIEGO, CALIFORNIA

YEAR FOUNDED: 2011

MISSION STATEMENT: Giving dogs the lives they deserve.

How many pets have you found homes for?

The Barking Lot has adopted out over 6,000 dogs and counting since 2011.

How do you ensure the pets go to a good home?

The Barking Lot has a stringent adoption screening process that includes a detailed questionnaire, a home check conducted by a volunteer, an in-person playdate, and an assessment by the director to match the potential adopter with the best dog for their needs.

Why should people adopt shelter pets instead of purchasing pets from stores or breeders?

As well as being wonderful companions, dogs are amazing teachers, and we've learned so much from them—first and foremost that they all deserve a chance at a better life, and their behavior will balance beautifully if their needs are met and good leadership is applied. These pups are the most grateful creatures you've ever encountered if given the right environment.

What do you love about this line of work?

We are a small organization with a handful of key volunteers, and we strive to find a great match for each pooch so that they'll be happy and have their needs fulfilled in their permanent "barking spots." Satisfied pups make for happy people when it comes to a forever home.

How did you start working with Sir Darius?

We met Sir Darius through our partnership with Soi Dog Foundation. Sir Darius visited our facility in Ramona, California (dubbed "The Ranch"), in June 2021 for a volunteer day, and we have been incorporating Beaux & Paws bow ties into adoption photos ever since.

What impact have Sir Darius's bow ties made on your adoptions?

The bow ties have added a fun and creative twist to help our rescue dogs get noticed! It really spiffs up their listing on our website and helps catch the eye of potential adopters.

How has Sir Darius's work impacted or inspired you?

We are huge fans of Sir Darius and are truly inspired and honored to work alongside him in our shared mission of helping shelter pets find homes and giving them the lives they deserve.

NAME: **KOOKY**

OWNER: **ADA**

BREED: **CHIHUAHUA**

AGE: **2**

ADOPTED FROM: **HEAVENLY ANGELS ANIMAL RESCUE**

DISLIKES: **SUDDEN NOISES**

LIKES: **SOFT TOYS**

What happened when you saw or met your dog for the first time?

It was immediate love.

How would you describe your dog's personality?

Kooky is just a very happy girl. She loves people, she loves to play with her toys, and, most importantly, she loves to cuddle with me. Amazing temperament, super smart, and so pretty.

How has your life changed since adopting your dog?

All my fur-babies are special, and Kooky is no different. She has brought me so much joy and laughter.

How has your dog's life changed since being adopted?

When Kooky came home, she was a little shy and reserved, but with lots of love and patience, she flourished into the happiest dog. She adjusted to our life and is now queen of the house.

How has Sir Darius's work impacted or inspired you?

I'm the co-chair and creative director of the New York Pet Fashion Show, where Sir Darius has made bow ties and unique outfits for rescue pets to model onstage. To see a young person care for others, especially animals, is definitely an inspiration. His passion for helping animals in need through such special talent and creativity is amazing.

Putting the "Cat" (and Dog) in Catwalk

Every year, the New York Pet Fashion Show showcases the hottest pet clothing and accessories—and raises money for the Mayor's Alliance for NYC's Animals. When I was ten, chairman Gregg Oehler and co-chair Ada Nieves invited me to join as the youngest designer in the event's history. That year's theme was "Made in America," and my assignment was to design a bow tie for a pup waiting to be adopted. With help from my big sister, I made a red, white, and blue bow tie, along with a hat made of felt, tulle, and rhinestones.

On the day of the show, as I entered the ballroom in Manhattan, I was amazed to see not only dogs but also cats, chickens, miniature horses, bearded lizards, and more, all wearing elaborate gowns, rhinestone-studded costumes, and exquisite headpieces. I had the honor of walking the catwalk with a handsome pup named Crosby, who was adopted after the event.

I was thrilled to be invited back the following year, which had a masquerade theme. For an adoptable pup named Butters, I created a blue rhinestoned bodice, a detachable blue-and-yellow tutu, and a sequin-trimmed mask with feathers. I wore a bow tie to match.

Sir Darius and Butters walk the runway.

The year after that, I created matching custom bow ties for myself and an adoptable dog named Zachary. To fit that year's sci-fi theme, I used a fabric with a purple-and-blue galaxy pattern and silver sequins.

The New York Pet Fashion Show had to pause for a few years because of the pandemic, but I hope to participate again soon so I can keep helping dogs find their FURever homes in a fun and unique way.

NAMES: **ROSIE AND STAR**

OWNER: **TERRIE**

BREEDS: **SHIH TZU MIX AND YORKSHIRE TERRIER**

AGES: **6 AND 4**

ADOPTED FROM: **DENVILLE ANIMAL SHELTER**

DISLIKES: **VACUUMS, BIG DOGS (ROSIE)**

LIKES: **EGGS, TV, PRINCE (ROSIE); DOG FRIENDS, LONG WALKS, TREATS, DAVID BOWIE (STAR)**

What were your dogs' lives like before being rescued?

Rosie was rescued from a case of animal hoarding where she was living in squalor with 275 other dogs in one small home. I saw the case on the news and heard that Denville Animal Shelter had taken in some of the dogs. When I saw her, I fell madly in love! She joined my family at nine weeks old. I think she still carries some trauma, as many things frighten her, but she is a loyal and fierce protector. When my sixteen-year-old dog Scarlet passed away, Rosie and I both had broken hearts. We weren't sure if we could love another dog. Then I heard about Star. Star came from a more common situation: her owner simply couldn't keep her. Star was three years old and weighed only five pounds when she was surrendered to the shelter. I heard about this tiny teacup Yorkie and brought Rosie to meet her. Star helped heal the pain of losing Scarlet, and now Rosie is happy to have another sister to pal around with.

What happened when you saw or met your dogs for the first time?
I run the Rock N' Ruff pet-adoption program at WDHA radio so I've worked with shelter dogs for many years. Meeting Rosie was different. It was love at first sight! With Star, I was grieving the loss of Scarlet, but I felt so bad for this tiny, lonely little girl who had no family. She broke my heart, and I knew I could give her the life she deserved.

How did you know these were the dogs for you?
Both of my girls really connected with me. It was really about the connection! And both fit my lifestyle with their unique personalities and small size.

How would you describe your dogs' personalities?
Rosie is a tough chick! She's nine pounds but would wrestle a bear to protect me. Very feisty! Star is laid-back and loves everyone and everything, especially her big sister, Rosie. They are so different in personality. It's really fun to have them around!

How has your life changed since adopting your dogs?
My life is fuller, richer, and way more fun since I adopted my girls. They are there in great times and hard times. They're loyal, comical, and great companions. I could not imagine my life without them.

How have your dogs' lives changed since being adopted?
If Rosie had stayed in that house of horrors, I don't know if she would have survived. Now she is the queen of the house and never has to worry about anything other than living her best life! Star was very shy of people's hands when I adopted her, so my guess is someone was "heavy-handed" and possibly hurt her. That is too hard for me to even think about. She will never have to worry about being mistreated again. They both have love to look forward to.

How has Sir Darius's work impacted or inspired you?
I've met Darius at Rock N' Ruff events, and he has always been a massive inspiration to me. Rosie has had one of his bow ties since I adopted her, and now we have one for Star too!

NAME: BELLA
OWNER: JOE
BREED: BEAGLE MIX
AGE: 2
ADOPTED FROM: ELEVENTH HOUR RESCUE
DISLIKES: THE IRONING BOARD, MY KAZOO, AND CEILING SHADOWS
LIKES: ADULTS, CHILDREN, OTHER DOGS

What was your dog's life like before being rescued?

Bella lived in North Carolina before she was transported to us here in New Jersey. Her first owner had a baby and felt that she could no longer properly care for Bella. Bella's second owner was a gentleman who couldn't spend enough time with her due to work. He asked a cat rescue person to please find Bella a good home.

What happened when you saw or met your dog for the first time?

My wonderful wife, Denise, saw Bella's photo on Eleventh Hour Rescue's website. She called me into our living room and announced, "Look at Bella, she's beautiful! Bella is our girl." We read Bella's biography, and she seemed to be a lot like Kelley, our rescue dachshund from Oklahoma, who had to be put to eternal rest a few months earlier after almost eight years together. Denise and I were grieving the loss of Kelley, and I cried almost every day until we met Bella. Since Bella loves people, she was very comfortable with us immediately when we met. I cuddled with her on our sofa only two hours after we adopted her.

How did you know this was the dog for you?

Bella's beautiful face made us fall in love with her as soon as we saw her. She appeared to be smiling in her photo, and she has gorgeous white teeth. Bella's personality profile was a perfect fit for us.

How would you describe your dog's personality?

Bella is very lovable and playful. She always wants to be with Denise or me when we're at home. She is extremely good at understanding simple commands and our mutual needs for affection. Bella is a tremendous cuddler and a generous kisser. She is a sweetheart.

How has your life changed since adopting your dog?

Although Denise and I still miss Kelley, having a gem like Bella has helped ease the pain we experienced losing our adorable dachshund. We feel that Kelley had her paws involved in this incredible adoption; Bella's former owner's last name is Kelly. I recently had hip replacement surgery, and walking Bella in our neighborhood has given me some of the exercise required by my physical therapist. You should see Bella enthusiastically greet Denise when she comes home from work each day. Bella is a godsend.

How has your dog's life changed since being adopted?

Bella's life has changed in that she has both a dad and a mom for the first time, without any children or any other pets. She gets to meet new people and travel when we get invited to visit friends and relatives in Vermont or the Jersey Shore. Bella will be going whenever we go.

How has Sir Darius's work impacted or inspired you?

We met Sir Darius when he was judging contests at a dog adoption event with WDHA radio, Eleventh Hour Rescue, and other pet rescue groups. He picked Kelley and me as the dog and owner who looked most alike! I bought a bow tie from Darius, because I knew that the proceeds went to animal shelters, and I wore it to an annual dinner to benefit people with ALS, where I received many compliments. Darius and his work are extremely inspiring. Denise, Bella, and I plan to attend as many dog adoption events as possible to show everyone that rescuing shelter animals is very rewarding.

Peanut sports a stylish Beaux & Paws bow tie at Mt. Pleasant Animal Shelter.

SHELTER NAME: MT. PLEASANT ANIMAL SHELTER

LOCATION: EAST HANOVER, NEW JERSEY

YEAR FOUNDED: 1972

MISSION STATEMENT: Our mission is to build a community of people and organizations working together to save today's—and prevent tomorrow's—abused, neglected, and homeless animals.

How many pets have you found homes for?
In total, about 40,000 animals, including 20,000 dogs.

How do you ensure the pets go to a good home?
We use a combination of adoption applications, vet checks, meet and greets, and adoption counselors.

Why should people adopt shelter pets instead of purchasing pets from stores or breeders?
About 6.5 million animals enter U.S. shelters annually. Of those, 1.5 million

end up being euthanized. It is also a very difficult time for shelters, with many having more animals than they can shelter. Adopting saves the life of one animal, which also means the shelter you adopt from can bring in a new animal to save. Mt. Pleasant Animal Shelter's adoption fee covers spay or neuter surgery for that pet, which pet stores do not do. Spaying/neutering improves health outcomes for your dog and prevents breeding, which is important because there are already more than enough shelter dogs who need homes! Many pets sold in pet stores come from puppy mills, where animals live in horrible conditions and often develop illnesses. Mt. Pleasant Animal Shelter places high importance on the medical care and behavioral training of each dog.

What do you love about this line of work?

Seeing animals leave the shelter with their new owners is amazing. It's incredible to see the actual smiles on the dogs' faces as they pose with their new owners for an adoption photo. My favorite thing is to see dogs who have had a long-term stay with us get adopted. The joy on all staff members' faces shows how invested we all are, not only in animal welfare but also in each individual animal we shelter.

How did you start working with Sir Darius?

Sir Darius has been providing bow ties for us for years, helping our pets get adopted. He has come to our shelter for media opportunities, joined in our annual Pet Palooza, and more. We are so thankful for our connection with Sir Darius.

What impact have Sir Darius's bow ties made on your adoptions?

The bow ties that Sir Darius creates show each dog's unique personality and accentuates their cuteness! The dogs love wearing them too—they're never bothered by them. The impact of these bow ties is what matters most: getting dogs adopted. When a dog goes home with a bow tie, the new owners also feel special and even more in love with their new, dapper pet.

How has Sir Darius's work impacted or inspired you?

Sir Darius is an amazing advocate for dogs, and he has such a kind and genuine heart. The work he's doing is incredible. Without voices, dogs need spokespeople to stand up for them. Most shelters are full of animals and low on funds and resources. The awareness Sir Darius brings to animal welfare, shelter needs, and homeless dogs is so admirable and valued!

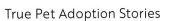

NAME: **ROSCOE**

OWNER: **PAULA**

BREED: **TREEING WALKER COONHOUND**

AGE: **4**

ADOPTED FROM: **MT. PLEASANT ANIMAL SHELTER**

DISLIKES: **LOUD NOISES**

LIKES: **TENNIS BALLS!**

What happened when you saw or met your dog for the first time?
He was very timid and scared, but he warmed up to us after about five minutes. (It helped that we had tennis balls!)

How did you know this was the dog for you?
My daughter bonded with him right away.

How would you describe your dog's personality?
He's quirky. Scared at first but very loving. When he's at the dog park, he's everyone's friend.

How has your life changed since adopting your dog?
Our lives are so much better! He's part of the family. We feel complete.

How has your dog's life changed since being adopted?
He's loved, cuddled, and taken care of!

NAME: MORTY
OWNER: DANIELLE
BREED: CHIHUAHUA
AGE: 7
ADOPTED FROM: LONG WAY HOME ADOPTABLES
DISLIKES: HUMAN FOOD, FRESH AIR
LIKES: CLOTHES, SOFT BLANKETS, BOSSING HUMANS AROUND

What was your dog's life like before being rescued?
We knew he was special needs. He was missing an eye and had neurological difficulties, but we didn't know how extensive it was before he arrived.

How did you know this was the dog for you?
He was so small and scared, and we loved him instantly.

How would you describe your dog's personality?
Bossy and full of love. He could rule the world with guilt trips alone.

How has your life changed since adopting your dog?
He's like our child. Everything we do revolves around him and his needs. He's very spoiled!

How has your dog's life changed since being adopted?
Morty was neglected for the first five years of his life and spent a lot of his time alone. Now he's the center of our world, and he's embraced it completely, making up for lost time and loneliness with love and snuggles and a whole laundry list of demands daily.

NAME: RIO
OWNER: KAREN
BREED: SHIH TZU
AGE: 6
ADOPTED FROM: ALBERT'S DOG LOUNGE
DISLIKES: VACUUMS, BROOMS
LIKES: PEOPLE, FOOD, SLEEP

What was your dog's life like before being rescued?

Rio was brought to a vet in Conroe, Texas, with severe health problems, including infected and damaged eyes. The owner couldn't pay for the needed surgeries and surrendered him. There was lots of debate on whether to save him or not. Two rescue groups stepped forward: Albert's Dog Lounge fostered him, and Friends of Faye raised money to pay for his surgeries. Rio lost both eyes at the young age of four. He was fostered by a wonderful family, and we found him on Petfinder.com.

What happened when you saw or met your dog for the first time?

He was in the arms of a volunteer after taking a very long ride in a van from Texas to Wisconsin. There were several other rescued dogs with him. I recognized him right away and, of course, fell in love.

How did you know this was the dog for you?

First of all, he fit all of my parameters (small, hypoallergenic, not a puppy). And then he was so adorable. I didn't even notice he had no eyes until I read his bio. I wasn't sure I could handle a blind dog. We hadn't had any dog for over thirty years. But after talking with the foster, I knew he was the one.

How would you describe your dog's personality?

So happy! Remarkable in his abilities to get around. Quiet, loyal, funny, brave, adaptable.

How has your life changed since adopting your dog?

He has become an officially licensed emotional support dog for my husband, Tom, who suffers from serious chronic health issues. He gives Tom such joy and comfort in a world where Tom has lost so much. Blind dogs can do most anything! We all adore each other, and we can't imagine life without him.

How has your dog's life changed since being adopted?

He has adapted to his blindness by learning new commands such as "step up," "step down," "stop," and "wait." He astounds most people with his abilities.

How has Sir Darius's work impacted or inspired you?

I believe in and support the mission! Please consider rescuing your pet. These animals don't deserve to be on the street or locked up in shelters. Brave and burned-out rescuers and fosters can help many more animals if the rest of us step up to adopt. You never know what miracles of joy and comfort can occur.

A PAWS Chicago pooch waiting to find a FURever home.

SHELTER NAME: PAWS CHICAGO

LOCATION: CHICAGO, ILLINOIS

YEAR FOUNDED: 1997

MISSION STATEMENT: To end the overpopulation of homeless animals through solutions, practices, and education, and to transform animal welfare by setting higher standards in the way animals are treated.

How many pets have you found homes for?

In 2022 we had nearly 5,000 adoptions, and we also served more than 25,000 animals. We provide low- and no-cost spay and neuter services and vaccines for pets, and we operate one of the largest dog and cat medical centers in the country.

How do you ensure the pets go to a good home?

PAWS Chicago employees and volunteers log every interaction with our animals and score them on several factors, from energy level to how they interact with other dogs or cats. We also have what we call the "comPETability test" on our website, so that potential adopters or fosters receive the best animal for their needs and current living situations.

Why should people adopt shelter pets instead of purchasing pets from stores or breeders?

With millions of homeless pets killed in the United States each year, it's hard to think of a good reason not to adopt! When you adopt, you save TWO lives—the life of the pet you're taking home and that of another who is now able to come into the adoption program. You just made room for the shelter to take in, and thereby save, another homeless pet.

What do you love about this line of work?

Who doesn't love saving the lives of dogs?

How did you start working with Sir Darius?

Sir Darius visited PAWS Chicago in August 2019, bow ties in hand, and visited with many of our adoptable pups. They loved sitting and playing with him, and his bow ties really made them stand out.

What impact have Sir Darius's bow ties made on your adoptions?

The bow ties are adorable on the dogs and really get the attention of people who might potentially adopt them. We also use them often for our Pet of the Week segments on local television stations—the additional "swag" attracts more attention to the dogs and increases the chances of finding a loving home that much quicker.

How has Sir Darius's work impacted or inspired you?

We salute anyone who wants to connect dogs with loving homes, but Sir Darius being such a handsome young entrepreneur gives us all an additional boost of energy. We salute his efforts, and we know he is headed for big things. He is a friend of PAWS Chicago for life!

NAME: **RAVEN**
OWNER: **NANCY**
BREED: **DOBERMAN**
AGE: **8**
ADOPTED FROM: **NORTH SMITHFIELD ANIMAL SHELTER**
DISLIKES: **CUCUMBERS**
LIKES: **EVERYTHING ELSE**

What happened when you saw or met your dog for the first time?

I used to have a shelter Doberman named Josh, who was a wonderful dog in every way. He passed away, but I still miss him. So I was happy to get Raven. I had waited a long time to get another Dobie, and it was awesome to have her in my home.

How did you know this was the dog for you?

All the Dobermans I've owned were meant for me!

How would you describe your dog's personality?

All-around great personality, always happy. She is so silly, and she loves life.

How has your life changed since adopting your dog?

Raven brings me so much joy.

How has your dog's life changed since being adopted?

I could tell she was going to enjoy living again. She went to training when she was young and did well—she still remembers her commands.

How has Sir Darius's work impacted or inspired you?

I am always inspired by my friend Sir Darius and what he does for the animals. My dog wears his bow ties. He's awesome! I hope more people give a shelter dog a chance at a new life—they will repay you over and over with love.

NAME: OLIVE
OWNER: ALEXANDRA
BREED: MUTT
AGE: 4.5
ADOPTED FROM: STRAY NETWORK ANIMAL RESCUE
DISLIKES: FALLING LEAVES, THE AMAZON DELIVERY GUY, HAIR DRYERS
LIKES: CHEESE, HUGS, DOGS ON TV, MOM'S BED, A STUFFED UNICORN
TOY WITH NO STUFFING LEFT, PLAYDATES WITH DOG FRIENDS

What was your dog's life like before being rescued?
Olive's mom was rescued from Mississippi while she was pregnant, so she was born in a foster home with the rescue group.

What happened when you saw or met your dog for the first time?
We had just lost our eight-year-old chocolate lab, Austyn, about a week prior. I was scrolling Facebook and randomly saw an ad for Stray Network. It was a picture of baby Olive, and I immediately knew I needed to meet her. Losing Austyn was so fresh, I wasn't looking for a dog at all, but—I know it sounds crazy—I think he sent her to us and knew we needed her in our world. Our home was quiet. There was a big void where he had been for so long, and we needed joy. We went to their adoption event, and when I went into the area where Olive and her siblings were, she came right up to me, climbed into my lap, and curled up. It was love at first cuddle.

How did you know this was the dog for you?
When you say "olive juice," your mouth moves exactly the same as when you say "I love you." I know I sound nuts, and maybe I am, but I felt like her name was even more of a sign!

How would you describe your dog's personality?
Quirky, laid-back, a bit shy, a big baby.

How has your life changed since adopting your dog?
She brought our house back to life.

How has your dog's life changed since being adopted?
She's a princess.

How has Sir Darius's work impacted or inspired you?
I was inspired to buy one of Sir Darius's bow ties for my fur-baby because I love that he also donates one to a shelter animal.

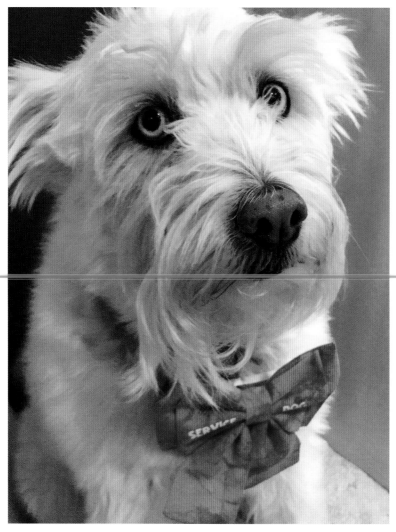

Angel, a Canine Support Teams' rescue who found a home as a beloved service dog.

SHELTER NAME: CANINE SUPPORT TEAMS

LOCATION: MURRIETA, CALIFORNIA

YEAR FOUNDED: 1989

MISSION STATEMENT: Our mission is to provide specially trained assistance/service dogs to people with disabilities to support their personal, social, and occupational independence.

How many pets have you found homes for?
We have trained over fifty shelter dogs to be service dogs since 1989.

How do you ensure the pets go to a good home?
Each client is interviewed, goes through a training process, and is followed up with annually.

Why should people adopt shelter pets instead of purchasing pets from stores or breeders?
Shelter dogs can make wonderful pets!

What do you love about this line of work?
Giving back to those in need. The service dogs change their owners' lives by providing them the gift of independence through the taskwork they've been trained to do. The companionship is equally important. Before having a service dog, our clients are often reliant on others, and many feel lonely, as their disabilities can often limit their experiences. These dogs allow them to do things more independently.

How has Sir Darius's work impacted or inspired you?
Darius has a heart of gold and is doing an amazing job using his skills for good. He lets people see the great personalities of these shelter dogs that might otherwise be missed. The bow ties make them really stand out.

NAME: SASHA
OWNER: LATISHA
BREED: PIT BULL
AGE: 12 WEEKS
DISLIKES: LOUD NOISES
LIKES: BALLS, SLIPPERS, CHEW TOYS, CHICKEN,
RUNNING AROUND THE YARD

What was your dog's life like before being rescued?

Her mother had several puppies, and they were going to be taken to a shelter because the owner could not care for all of them.

What happened when you saw or met your dog for the first time?

Meeting Sasha was like seeing a newborn child for the first time. I instantly fell in love. We had a lot of physical contact: she climbed up on my body and licked my face. She was the sweetest and most precious pup.

How did you know this was the dog for you?

I picked her up, and I just knew she had to be mine.

How would you describe your dog's personality?

Sasha is fun, energetic, loving, and affectionate.

How has your life changed since adopting your dog?

I am a lot happier since Sasha came into my life. My two daughters are happier, and they love Sasha so much. They're learning how to be responsible by helping me take care of Sasha. She is our little angel.

How has your dog's life changed since being adopted?

Sasha was going to be taken to a shelter, but now she has a forever home and is a very happy pup.

How has Sir Darius's work impacted or inspired you?

He is a very inspiring young man. I never wanted a dog, but after a few years of following Sir Darius, I was convinced to bring a dog into my home. Rescuing or adopting a dog is one of the most selfless things you can do. Not only are you saving a dog's life and providing them with a home, but dogs bring so much fun, warmth, and happiness into your life as well.

NAME: CUBBIE
OWNER: LAURIE
BREED: TERRIER/PAPILLON MIX
AGE: 7
ADOPTED FROM: CARSON ANIMAL SHELTER
DISLIKES: LEAF BLOWERS, SQUIRRELS, BATHS
LIKES: HER STUFFED TOY GUMBY, CHICKEN JERKY TREATS, CHASING LIZARDS

What was your dog's life like before being rescued?
She was a stray, wandering the streets, and picked up by animal control at about eight months old.

What happened when you saw or met your dog for the first time?
I'd been looking online and going to shelters and rescues. I trusted that when I was the right fit for a dog, I would know it. One day, Cubbie's picture appeared on the shelter's Facebook page, and I felt like she was looking right at me. She was shaved and scrawny and had such a funny face. It was like I'd already known her and she was just waiting for me. I immediately called the shelter and put my name down for an adoption application, then drove over to meet her.

How did you know this was the dog for you?

Many of the dogs at the shelter were stressed out, barking, growling, or withdrawn, but Cubbie was standing there wagging her tail and had a big happy smile. She looked like she was just ready to come home. She walked over and stood on her hind legs and licked my hand. It was a magical moment, and I had no doubt that I was going to be her dog mom.

How would you describe your dog's personality?

Cubbie is a very high-energy, frisky, mischievous dog. She always makes us laugh. She's bold, protective, and loyal. She can be jealous of other animals. She never really bonded with my cat and she still doesn't get along with our tortoise, but she is, like all dogs, made of love. She wants to love all humans and can charm anyone into loving her.

How has your life changed since adopting your dog?

I've lived with quite a few wonderful animals who somehow drifted into my life. I never went out looking to adopt until Cubbie. The process of finding her took me into the shelter system, and that was an eye-opener. Cubbie is a precious family member, and it's sad to think of how her life started out. But it's also a source of gratitude to know she was saved from the streets and was able to find us. As well as being my beloved companion, she's opened my heart more to all dogs. I started volunteering in shelters since this adoption experience so I could have a small part in helping the plight of homeless animals.

How has your dog's life changed since being adopted?

Instead of concrete to sleep on, she's got pink velvet cushions. All her fur grew back. She gets a new toy for holidays and birthdays. She gets home-cooked food, and she gets to spend her days chasing quails and lizards in a safe backyard.

How has Sir Darius's work impacted or inspired you?

I was so heartened and inspired to learn about this young person having the inspiration and initiative to use his time and talent in such a compassionate project, so of course we purchased one of his bow ties for Cubbie. There are so many animals—feral cat colonies, homeless dogs. They can't fend for themselves. They need support and care from humans to survive. They give so much in return for a little human kindness: love, loyalty, joy, steadfast companionship. Thank you, Sir Darius Brown, for all of your good work. We look forward to seeing what you do next.

NAME: LACY
OWNER: AVA (OF AVA'S PET PALACE)
BREED: MINIATURE PINSCHER MIX
AGE: 15
ADOPTED FROM: MAGNIFICENT MUTTS RESCUE
DISLIKES: WATER, THE VACUUM, THE DOORBELL
LIKES: SALMON TREATS, CUDDLING, SNORING LOUDLY, BELLY RUBS

What was your dog's life like before being rescued?

All we know about Lacy before she came to us was that she was found in Kentucky and that she had given birth to two puppies. We have assumed other things about her past based on the way she acts and the different quirks she has. All I know now is that we're so happy to have

her here with us as a part of our family, making so many memories!

What happened when you saw or met your dog for the first time?

When I first met Lacy, I wasn't sure what to expect, as the other dogs we'd fostered were playful puppies and a very spontaneous Jack Russell terrier; Lacy was the first dog we fostered that was nervous to be around us and hadn't had much experience around people in general. I knew from the moment I met her that we would be best friends, and we sure are! I couldn't be more thankful for the joy and unconditional love Lacy has brought us.

How did you know this was the dog for you?

I knew Lacy was the dog for us almost right when we met her. She was very timid, but after we'd fostered her for three or four weeks, she warmed up to us and became the sweetest dog ever. I knew that how much she'd grown in that short amount of time was a big milestone, and I wanted Lacy to be a part of our family. Everyone in our family knew Lacy was meant to be our dog, and every aspect of the adoption worked out perfectly.

How would you describe your dog's personality?

I would say Lacy's personality is similar to mine. She is a laid-back and reserved dog for the most part. She has her moments where she may see another dog and kind of go crazy, but other than that, she's a very chill, loving, and super cute pup. She has been the perfect fit for our family.

How has your life changed since adopting your dog?

Lacy has changed our lives in such a positive way! Lacy is the first dog I've had to take care of permanently, and it's been such a learning experience going on adventures with her, snuggling with her, having her taste-test all of my treats, and so much more. I'm so happy that Lacy came into my life. She's been such a positive influence on me.

How has your dog's life changed since being adopted?

I would say that Lacy's life has definitely changed in a positive way since she came to us. We don't know much about her past, but she does certain things that show she did not live in a good environment before we adopted her. She was a very timid dog who was often scared to eat around us or even let us pet her, but now she is very bright, happy, and loved. She is also very protective of me and has been this way for the past few years.

How has Sir Darius's work impacted or inspired you?

I would say that adopting a pet instead of buying one is important, as there are so many animals out there who need loving homes and families. It is so important that we do what we can to help support these shelters saving so many animals' lives. We can do this by donating, volunteering (which I love to do!), and fostering. I'm a really big rescue advocate who stands by the saying "Adopt, don't shop."

This pup from Fetcher Dog has found a loving FURever home.

SHELTER NAME: FETCHER DOG

LOCATION: KENT, ENGLAND

YEAR FOUNDED: 2018

MISSION STATEMENT: We rescue 100 dogs per year from kill shelters and the streets of Bosnia and beyond. We care for their welfare in our kennels and find forever homes for them in the UK.

How many pets have you found homes for?

Six hundred.

How do you ensure the pets go to a good home?

All of our adopters go through an extensive application procedure that includes a pre-adoption form, a home check, and a meeting with one of our founders.

Why should people adopt shelter pets instead of purchasing pets from stores or breeders?

There are so many dogs of all shapes, sizes, breeds, and ages sitting in rescues and shelters all around the world. There seems to be a misconception that all dogs from rescues are damaged in some way, and that is simply not true. If you have specific requirements, I can guarantee there is a dog matching your needs sitting in a rescue waiting for a home—you just have to look.

What do you love about this line of work?

We love the transformations from rescue to forever home. We see dogs literally on the brink of death, and then we see that same dog lounging on someone's sofa a few months later, as if nothing bad had ever happened to them.

How did you start working with Sir Darius?

In 2018, we were just getting off the ground, and we reached out to Sir Darius on Instagram, as we had seen the incredible work he was doing for rescue dogs and thought his bow ties might help our dogs find forever homes of their own. He did not hesitate to share us on his social media platforms and make bow ties for our dogs. We were the first rescue in England that he sent bow ties to, so it was very exciting for us!

What impact have Sir Darius's bow ties made on your adoptions?

It's something a little fun and different that we can do to highlight the dogs that need homes. Anything that we can do to make the dogs stand out is beneficial, and the bow ties certainly do that.

How has Sir Darius's work impacted or inspired you?

Both Sir Darius and his mom are so passionate about helping rescue dogs. Despite school and work commitments, they have continued to support so many animals and raise awareness of dog adoption not only in the U.S. but here in England too. We are just so grateful for everything you do for rescue dogs around the world. So, from the dogs, we thank you.

NAME: JAX AND GIGI
OWNER: SYLVA
BREED: JINDO MIX
AGE: 7
ADOPTED FROM: ADOPT-A-DOG ANIMAL SHELTER
DISLIKES: THE VACUUM, SQUIRRELS, BICYCLE RIDERS, BEING LEFT
HOME ALONE, ANIMALS ON TV
LIKES: CHICKEN, STEAK, SQUEAKY TOYS, COD-SKIN TREATS, GOING TO
THE PARK, RUNNING, PLAYING, GOING IN THE CAR

What were your dogs' lives like before being rescued?
Jax and Gigi are a brother and sister from the same litter. The rescue nicknamed them the Miracle Family because they were able to save all four puppies in the litter and their mother from a bad situation—a miracle!

What happened when you saw or met your dogs for the first time?
From the moment we were given permission to adopt them, I was already in love. I loved them even before I met them. I prepared for their long-awaited arrival by setting up their crates with bedding, toys, treats, and anything else I could think of. My house looked like a pink and blue explosion. Excitement, nervousness, and pure elation are the emotions I felt leading up to the day of the adoption, but on that day, the only emotion that mattered was love!

How did you know these were the dogs for you?

I showed my husband the video and pictures of the Miracle Family on Facebook. He took one look at Gigi's face and said, "I have to have that dog." We soon got the OK to adopt "the brown dog," but I couldn't help but ask my husband, "Do you want to get the white one too?" And the rest is history, as they say. Your heart just knows when you find the one. We needed to give them a home where they would never have to fear anyone or anything ever again.

How would you describe your dogs' personalities?

Jax is a very silly boy who loves being told that he did a good job. He's a big baby and a gentle giant who loves to carry around his toys. He loves to give his mommy "hugs" and has been known to "French kiss" way too many unsuspecting friends! His sister Gigi is an energetic tomboy. She's tough as nails, not afraid of anything, always wanting to play with her brother. But mostly, she is the apple of her daddy's eye. Jax and Gigi both are so loyal, loving, funny, silly, and oh so happy!

How has your life changed since adopting your dogs?

I know it might sound corny or dramatic to some people, but our life is now complete. Basically, we try to incorporate them into our daily lives as much as possible.

Although it is a lot of responsibility, the rewards far outweigh the sacrifices. I will happily do without if it means that my pups get the healthiest food, best veterinary care, etc. I will forever be grateful to them, and, of course, the rescuer and shelter.

How has your dogs' lives changed since being adopted?

My pups were living in a disgusting rusted cage with no padding on the bottom, eating waste from restaurants that was covered in maggots. They were truly living in a hell on earth, and had it not been for all the people who worked together to rescue them, they would not be living the dream life they have now.

How has Sir Darius's work impacted or inspired you?

I wish the world was filled with more bright, compassionate, kindhearted, entrepreneurial people like Sir Darius. He is using his talents to help make a difference in the lives of pets in need. I want to thank Sir Darius for being a solid role model for both the young and old. We need to show the world that rescue dogs are wonderful. From my experience, there is nothing better than a rescue dog, because they somehow know that you saved them, and in turn, they show you every day just how grateful they are.

NAME: **SASHA**

OWNER: **JESS**

BREED: **RUSSIAN BLUE**

AGE: **5**

ADOPTED FROM: **CITY CRITTERS**

DISLIKES: **LOUD NOISES, TUMMY RUBS, NOT BEING THE CENTER OF ATTENTION**

LIKES: **HAIR TIES, MOUSE TOYS, CATNIP, SLICED TURKEY**

What was your cat's life like before being rescued?

Sasha was rescued in Brooklyn, New York, when she was six months old. She was wandering around a side street and approached a complete stranger who just so happened to work for an animal rescue. It appeared that Sasha had escaped from her previous home somehow or was left out by an owner who did not go looking for her. She was cold and hungry and in need of a loving home. That's when the City Critters animal rescue took her in to help find her a new family to provide endless love and care for her.

What happened when you saw or met your cat for the first time?

It was love at first sight when we first met Sasha! She was so warm and affectionate, and came over to us right away. We knew she was the perfect fit for our family and fell in love immediately.

How did you know this was the cat for you?

We knew Sasha was the cat for us because of her friendly and warm demeanor. She let us pick her up and cuddle her almost immediately.

How would you describe your cat's personality?

Sasha is affectionate, loving, playful, smart, and very sweet.

How has your life changed since adopting your cat?

Sasha has changed our life completely. She was like my husband's and my first child together. Sasha has moved with us from NYC to New Jersey, where we now are in our forever home. We also now have a human baby who just turned one, and we feel like our family is almost complete!

How has your cat's life changed since being adopted?

Sasha was in need of us as much as we were in need of her! She has grown into a beautiful, smart, loving, and wise cat. She is so happy to be part of our family.

How has Sir Darius's work impacted or inspired you?

Pet rescue and adoption are important because there are so many animals out there who need a loving home. Otherwise, they face a challenging life and even euthanasia. We must do everything we can to help these animals and give them the lives they deserve.

NAME: KEEGAN
OWNERS: MARA AND CAMERON
BREED: GERMAN SHEPHERD MIX
AGE: 4
ADOPTED FROM: NIAGARA DOG RESCUE
DISLIKES: BATHS, WAITING FOR DINNER, LONG CAR RIDES
LIKES: TREATS, SNOW, FAMILY WALKS, TUG-OF-WAR

What was your dog's life like before being rescued?
He was a stray before ending up in a shelter in Kentucky. From there, he was rescued from the euthanasia list by Niagara Dog Rescue. He waited a long time and stayed with a few different kennels and fosters before finally finding his forever family here in Canada.

What happened when you saw or met your dog for the first time?
We absolutely fell in love with Keegan from the first time we met him. He was so

excited and full of energy and constantly had a big goofy grin on his face. It was hard to have to say goodbye, but we knew we would be back to pick him up a few weeks later and bring him home with us.

How did you know this was the dog for you?

We had considered a few dogs through the rescue when our adoption lead suggested that Keegan might be the perfect pup for us. When we first met him, we stopped to rest after a long walk and Keegan sat right on Cameron's foot. We knew then that he'd chosen us to be his family. He still sits on our feet to this day.

How would you describe your dog's personality?

Keegan is a playful goof. He's easily distracted and a bit absent-minded and almost always has a doggy smile on his face. He lets us know it's playtime by enthusiastically "booping" us with his nose wherever he can reach, or by bringing one of his favorite toys to us to play tug-of-war. He's excited to meet new people and absolutely loves attention. He can also be lazy and enjoys a good nap.

How has your life changed since adopting your dog?

We became those people who get a dog and it becomes their personality. Our house is covered in fur and dog beds and toys. We base our plans around whether we can bring Keegan along or if we need a doggy-sitter. And we spend way too much money on fancy snacks and outfits for our special baby. And we wouldn't have it any other way!

How has your dog's life changed since being adopted?

We don't know too much about Keegan's life pre-adoption, but we know it wasn't ideal. He spent a lot of time alone and faced a lot of rejection on his journey to adoption. Now he's the spoiled only child of parents who love to shower him with love and attention.

How has Sir Darius's work impacted or inspired you?

While we didn't see Keegan on Sir Darius's platforms, we did follow Sir Darius on Instagram and knew about his amazing work helping animals find their forever homes. We knew that when we finally got our fur-baby, we would need to get him some bow ties. There are so many amazing animals waiting in shelters and kennels and foster homes for the opportunity to call a forever family their own. These animals are so smart and sweet and deserving of a loving home. They just need somebody to take a chance on them!

Justice waits to be adopted from Humane Animal Partners.

SHELTER NAME: HUMANE ANIMAL PARTNERS

LOCATION: THREE LOCATIONS IN DELAWARE

YEAR FOUNDED: Delaware Humane Association was founded in 1957, and Delaware Society for the Prevention of Cruelty to Animals was founded in 1873! In 2022, we merged to become Humane Animal Partners.

MISSION STATEMENT: Humane Animal Partners is committed to connecting people with animals, building strong relationships to better the community, and preventing cruelty to animals. These pillars are brought to life through programs that provide shelter and adoption for unwanted and homeless pets, reduce pet overpopulation through affordable spay/neuter, and enable pet retention by providing low-cost veterinary services.

How many pets have you found homes for?

We've been conducting our animal life-saving work for over 200 years, so...a lot!

How do you ensure the pets go to a good home?

We focus on finding the best fit possible for our animals. People interested in adopting complete a comprehensive adoption questionnaire that asks an array of lifestyle questions. From there, our experienced adoption counselors reach out and recommend the best animal possible for each person's unique lifestyle. This process has led to thousands of happy, beautiful adoptions. Our true power doesn't lie in just the numbers, though— it's our tailored approach to matchmaking. Our staff is proud to devote time, energy, and love to ensure they know every animal in our care by name. And when the right match is made, we strive to conduct our adoptions thoughtfully, transparently, and with the utmost respect.

Why should people adopt shelter pets instead of purchasing pets from stores or breeders?

Above all else, shelter pets are deserving and grateful. There are countless shelter animals out there at this very moment just waiting to be adopted and find a family of their own, and their stories are always incredible, no matter where they started. When you save the life of a shelter pet, you're saving the lives of many others by opening up space at the shelter for them.

What do you love about this line of work?

Where do we begin? The stories, the connections, the look on both an animal's and a human's face when they see each other and know they've found their match.

How did you start working with Sir Darius?

We saw Sir Darius on the *Today* show years ago and were so moved by his mission to help dogs get adopted. Fast forward a few years, and President Joe Biden adopted a dog from us! To celebrate the first ever shelter dog making its way to the White House, we hosted the virtual "indoguration" of Major Biden with Pumpkin Pet Insurance [see page 31]. We knew right away we wanted Sir Darius to be involved with such a special day, so we reached out and began working together. The rest is history!

What impact have Sir Darius's bow ties made on your adoptions?

Our staff loves styling our adoptable dogs (and cats!) in Sir Darius's bow ties. There's no doubt that our dogs look more dapper in a Beaux & Paws bow tie!

How has Sir Darius's work impacted or inspired you?

Sir Darius is a champion for the underdog. His empathy and compassion for animals is deeply moving. The world needs more young people like Sir Darius.

Chapter 3

Make a Bow Tie for Pets

Want to make your very own bow tie for a shelter pet or a furry friend? This chapter will teach you how! If you know how to use a sewing machine, turn to page 88 for instructions on how to sew a bow tie. If you don't know how to use a sewing machine, don't worry! Turn to page 98 for instructions on how to make a snazzy bow tie using glue instead of a needle and thread.

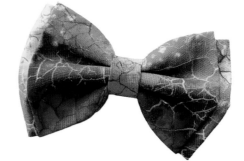

How to Sew a Bow Tie

Would your dog or cat look extra adorable in a bow tie? If you know how to use a sewing machine, you can use these instructions to sew your own! I'll break it down step by step so it's easy to follow along.

Materials

One 10" x 6" rectangle of 100% cotton fabric, in a pattern of your choice

One 5" x 3" rectangle of fabric in the same pattern

One 10" x 6" rectangle of interfacing fabric

An iron

A sewing machine with needle (not shown)

Thread

Two 2" pieces of elastic

Scissors

Thread nipper

Hand sewing needle (not shown)

1 Iron the large (10" x 6") fabric rectangle and the small (5" x 3") fabric rectangle to get rid of any wrinkles. Set the small rectangle aside for now.

2 Turn the large fabric rectangle over so the pattern is facedown on the ironing board. Lay the interfacing fabric on top of it and iron them to fuse them together.

TIP
The interfacing will keep your bow tie stiff so it stays in great shape over time!

3 Fold the fabric in half horizontally, with the interfacing on the outside.

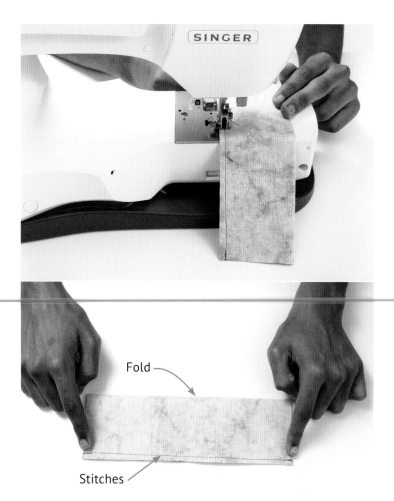

Fold

Stitches

4 Using a straight stitch, sew the unfolded ends together vertically on your sewing machine. Make sure to backstitch at the beginning and the end. Your fabric should now be in the shape of a tube with a fold along one edge and stitches along the other edge.

5 Turn the tube of fabric inside out so that the pattern is on the outside. Lay it flat on an ironing board and iron it to remove any wrinkles.

6 Fold your fabric in half horizontally to make a crease down the middle of the tube, then unfold it again.

7 Fold the left and right edges of the tube inward so they meet at the crease you made in the previous step. Make sure the two flaps of fabric don't overlap each other.

8 Iron to remove any wrinkles and crease the folds. You have now created two panels, one on the right and one on the left. These will be the left and right sides of the bow tie.

9 Unfold the panels so you have a long rectangular tube of fabric again. Lay it vertically on the sewing machine. Place one piece of elastic in the center of the right panel and sew each side of it down using a zigzag stitch. Repeat with the other piece of elastic on the left panel.

TIP In the final step, you'll slide a dog collar through these elastic straps. Make sure to leave enough room for your collar of choice to fit!

10 After attaching the elastic, use the thread nippers to snip off any excess thread on both panels.

11 Fold the panels in toward the center again. Using your sewing machine, sew a straight stitch securing the right panel to the center of the fabric. Repeat with the left panel.

12 Snip off the excess thread on both sides.

13 Fold your fabric in half horizontally so the elastic strips are visible on the outside of the fold.

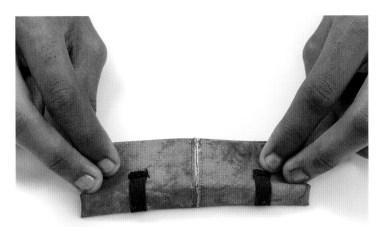

14 Fold the edge of the uppermost panel back toward the fold with the elastic on it (kind of like you're folding a paper airplane).

15 Keeping the fold from the previous step in place, flip your bow tie over and repeat on the other side.

16 Cut a generous piece of thread. Wrap it tightly around the middle of the bow tie several times and tie it off to create the iconic bow tie shape.

17 Take the small (5" x 3") rectangle that you set aside earlier and fold it in half horizontally.

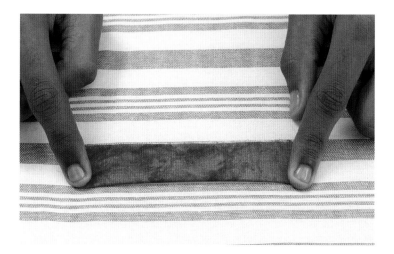

18 Iron to remove any wrinkles and crease the fold. This is what I call the "middle strip," which loops around the middle of your bow tie.

19 Fold one end of the middle strip around the middle of your bow tie.

20 Holding the bow tie with one hand, loop the middle strip all the way around and use the scissors to cut off any excess fabric.

21 Use a threaded needle to sew the middle strip into a closed loop, securing the middle of the bow tie.

22 Your bow tie is done! This is what it looks like from the front.

23 Slide a collar through the elastic loops on the back of the bow tie, and you're ready to make your dog or cat look dapper!

How to Make a Bow Tie with Fabric Glue

No sewing machine? No worries! With these step-by-step instructions, you can make a bow tie using fabric glue (or a hot glue gun with adult supervision) instead of a needle and thread.

Materials

One 10" x 6" rectangle of 100% cotton fabric, in a pattern of your choice

One 5" x 3" rectangle of fabric in the same pattern

One 10" x 6" rectangle of interfacing fabric

An iron

Fabric glue or a glue gun

Scissors

An elastic hair tie (ponytail holder)

1 Iron the large (10" x 6") fabric rectangle and the small (5" x 3") fabric rectangle. Set the small rectangle aside for now.

2 Turn the large fabric rectangle over so the pattern is facedown on the ironing board. Lay the interfacing fabric on top of it and iron them to fuse them together.

TIP
The interfacing will keep your bow tie stiff so it stays in great shape over time!

3 Fold the fabric in half horizontally, with the interfacing on the inside, to make a crease down the middle of the rectangle.

4 Unfold the fabric into a rectangle again. Fold the bottom edge of the rectangle upward to meet the crease you just made in the middle. Repeat with the top edge, making sure the two edges don't overlap each other.

5 Iron to crease the folds and make sure the fabric lies flat.

6 With the top and bottom edges still folded in toward the middle, fold your fabric in half vertically to make a crease in the center, perpendicular to the crease you made in step 3.

7 Fold the left and right edges of the fabric inward so they meet at the crease you made in the previous step.

8 Iron again to crease the folds and make sure the fabric lies flat. You have now created two panels, one on the left and one on the right. These will be the left and right sides of the bow tie.

9 Unfold the left panel and use your fabric glue or glue gun to lay a thin line of glue along the edge.

10 Fold the left panel back toward the center crease and press down to glue it in place, applying pressure for about 15 seconds. Repeat the process on the right side, making sure the two flaps of fabric don't overlap each other.

11 Fold the fabric in half horizontally, just like you did in step 3, except now you're working with a smaller rectangle.

12 Fold the edge of the uppermost panel back so it touches the fold you created in step 11 (kind of like you're folding a paper airplane).

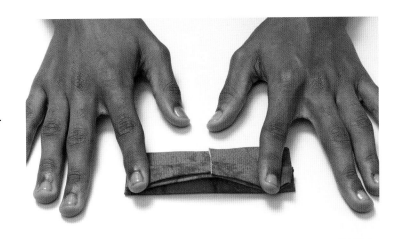

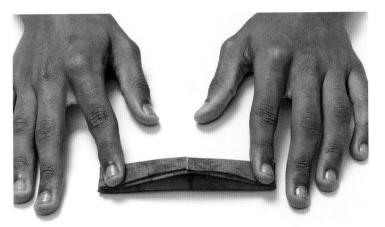

13 Keeping the fold from the previous step in place, flip your bow tie over and repeat on the other side.

14 Pinching the bow tie in the middle, pick it up. Open your fingers slightly and add a generous dollop of glue to the center of that fold (but don't overdo it!). Pinch tightly for about 15 seconds, until the glue is dry enough to hold the fabric in place, creating the iconic bow tie shape.

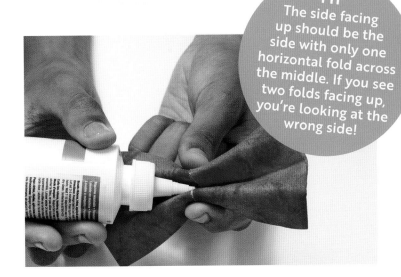

TIP
The side facing up should be the side with only one horizontal fold across the middle. If you see two folds facing up, you're looking at the wrong side!

15 Continuing to pinch the bow tie in the middle, flip it over to the opposite side. You should now see two horizontal folds across the middle of the bow tie. Add a dollop of glue to the center of both the upper fold and the lower fold, but DO NOT PINCH SHUT YET.

16 Press the elastic hair tie into the two glued folds, making sure it's centered evenly. Pinch tightly for about 15 seconds, until the glue is dry enough to hold the fabric in place.

TIP
This is the back of your bow tie. You'll use the elastic hair tie to secure the bow tie to a dog collar in the final step.

17 Take the smaller fabric rectangle you set aside earlier and fold it in thirds horizontally so that one flap overlaps the other.

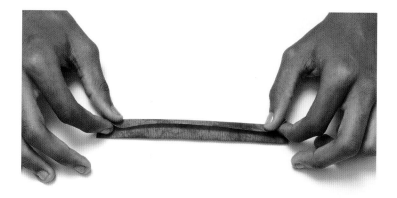

18 Add a thin line of glue along the lower flap.

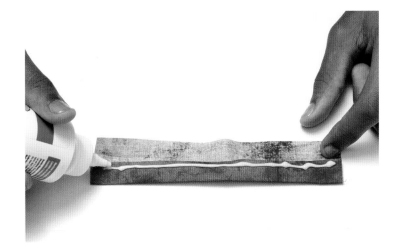

19 Press the upper flap over the lower flap and apply pressure for about 15 seconds. You've now created what I call the "middle strip," which will loop around the middle of your bow tie.

20 Lay the middle strip down vertically on the table. Place the bow tie facedown on top of it about one-third of the way down the strip.

21 Add a dot of glue to the center of the bow tie. Fold the top portion of the middle strip onto it. Apply pressure for about 15 seconds.

22 Use scissors to cut the excess fabric off the bottom portion of the middle strip.

23 Fold a small portion of the bottom of the middle strip upward and glue it in place, applying pressure for about 15 seconds. (This hides the ragged edge created by cutting off excess fabric in the previous step.)

24 Put a dot of glue in the center of the bow tie. Glue the bottom portion of the middle strip in place so it forms a closed loop around the middle of the bow tie, applying pressure for about 15 seconds.

25 Your bow tie is done! Here's what it looks like from the front.

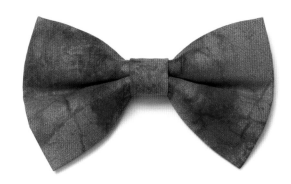

26 Slide a collar through the elastic loops formed by the hair tie, and you're ready to make your dog or cat look dapper!

Animal Shelters

Below is a list of shelters and rescue organizations I've worked with or donated bow ties to. If you're looking for a shelter to adopt from, volunteer at, or donate to, this list is a great place to start!

Alabama
Humane Society Pet Rescue & Adoption Center

Alaska
Alaska SPCA

Arizona
Camp Golden Years

Arkansas
Jacksonville Animal Shelter

California
Animal Friends of the Valleys
The Barking Lot
Canine Support Teams
Wagmor Pets

Colorado
Dumb Friends League

Connecticut
Lucky Dog Refuge

Delaware
Humane Animal Partners

District of Columbia
Humane Rescue Alliance

Florida
Orange County Animal Services
Tri-County Animal Rescue
Urgent Dogs and Cats of Miami

Georgia
One Love Animal Rescue

Hawaii
Hawaii Island Humane Society

Idaho
MCPAWS Regional Animal Shelter

Illinois
The Anti-Cruelty Society
PAWS Chicago

Indiana
Gibson County Animal Shelter

Iowa
Cedar Bend Humane Society

Kansas
Always and Furever Midwest Animal Sanctuary

Kentucky
Humane Society of Henderson County

Louisiana
Villalobos Rescue Center

Maine
Animal Refuge League of Greater Portland

Maryland
The Baltimore Animal Rescue and Care Shelter (BARCS)

Massachusetts
Last Hope K9 Rescue

Michigan
Detroit Animal Care and Control
Michigan Humane

Minnesota
Safe Hands Rescue

Mississippi
Southern Pines Animal Shelter

Missouri
KC Pet Project

Montana
Stafford Animal Shelter

Nebraska
Kearney Area Animal Shelter

Nevada
The Animal Foundation

New Hampshire
Hearts and Tails Animal Alliance
Manchester Animal Shelter

New Jersey
Associated Humane Societies
Jersey Shore Animal Center
Liberty Humane Society
Monmouth County SPCA
Mt. Pleasant Animal Shelter
St. Hubert's Animal Welfare Center

New Mexico
Sante Fe Animal Shelter

New York
Animal Haven
Muddy Paws Rescue
ASPCA
Bideawee
Long Island Bulldog Rescue
Mayor's Alliance of NYC's
  Animals
Rock n' Rescue

North Carolina
Montgomery County Animal
  Shelter

North Dakota
Homeward Animal Shelter

Ohio
Toledo Animal Rescue

Oklahoma
OKC Animal Welfare

Oregon
Oregon Humane Society

Pennsylvania
Philly PAWS
Street Tails Animal Rescue

Rhode Island
Providence Animal Rescue

South Carolina
Charleston Animal Society

South Dakota
Almost Home Canine Rescue

Tennessee
Nashville Humane Association

Texas
Houston PetSet
San Antonio Pets Alive

Utah
South Utah Valley Animal
  Shelter

Vermont
Humane Society of
  Chittenden County

Virginia
Gray Face Acres Senior
  Dog Rescue
Prince William County
  Animal Shelter

Washington
Whatcom Humane Society

Wisconsin
Underdog Pet Rescue

Wyoming
Cheyenne Animal Shelter

National
Pilots N Paws

International
Alberta Animal Rescue Crew
  Society (Canada)
Dogs Trust Ireland (Ireland)
Fetcher Dog (UK)
K9 Friends (UAE)
Shanghai Animal Rescue
  (China)
Soi Dog Foundation
  (Thailand/USA)

Acknowledgments

I want to thank those who have supported me and helped me get where I am today.

My mother, Joy Brown: Because of you, I am. Thank you for molding and shaping me into the young man I am today. There will never be enough hugs, thanks, or words to express my gratitude for all the sacrifices you've made by putting aside your dreams and goals to support all of mine. I am incredibly grateful for your unconditional love and for always believing in me.

My sister, Dazhai Brown: Thank you for teaching me how to sew bow ties and for being my best friend. Our bond is like no other and can never be broken. I love you and Mom both to infinity and beyond!

My father, Darius Brown Sr.: I remember when I was a very young boy, despite my challenges, you called me a scholar. You told me I was different and was destined to do great things in the world. You were right! Thank you for your encouragement and for seeing the greatness in me.

My grandmothers, Alice Dillard and Judy Catchens: Thank you for your love and affection. You both have continuously given so much of yourselves, and I am fortunate to have two thoughtful, caring, witty, loving grandmothers.

My great-grandparents Freddie and Lena Brown: I know you're looking down, watching over me, and always by my side.

I hope I'm making you proud.

Thabiti Boone: You were the first person aside from family and friends to purchase a custom bow tie from me and later became my mentor. Thank you for pouring so much into me and for being a strong male role model. You've helped change the trajectory of my life, and I'm forever indebted to you.

President Barack Obama: You showed up at a very important time at the beginning of this journey. Thank you for rooting for me, for your support, and for believing in me.

North Star Academy Charter School (Newark Liberty & Central): It takes a village, they say. Thank you to all my teachers for challenging, nurturing, and pushing me to reach my full potential.

Kelsea Little and the GoFundMe team: Thank you for choosing me as a GoFundMe Kid Hero, for your support of the PAWSome Mission, and for assembling a team to accompany me for a volunteer day at The Barking Lot in Ramona,

California. I'm forever grateful.

Singer Corporation and Windham Fabrics: Thank you for your support and partnership in providing me with the supplies needed to grow my business and to continue the PAWsome Mission.

Ada Nieves and Gregg Oehler: Thank you for the opportunity to be a designer at the New York Pet Fashion Show. You helped me step out of my comfort zone and introduced me to the world of pet fashion couture.

Robert Keszey: One message from you helped change my life. Thank you!

Andrea Stark: Thank you for acknowledging the work I do for shelter pets and for supporting and believing in me when others did not.

Allan Houston, Jelonda Foster, Rayshawna Frazier, and Antoinette Jennings: Thanks for supporting me and my business, and for the opportunity to deliver some of my first keynote speeches!

Darrell Edmonds of Friday Is Tie Day: Thank you for the opportunity to make an impact and help motivate other young men to become changemakers.

Dr. Sonia White of the S.M.I.L.E. Foundation: Your support means the world to me, and I greatly appreciate you.

Thank you to the Disney Dreamers Academy, Points of Light, the Prudential Spirit of Community Awards, PETA, and the Global Child Prodigy Awards for recognizing my work.

Thank you to the entire Soho team for the opportunity to write my first book and to all the individuals, shelters, and organizations who contributed. I'm honored to share all your adoptions, rescue stories, and missions with the world.

To my family, friends, supporters, partners, and all of my social media FURiends: I love you all. Thank you for believing in me. I am so grateful for all the support, encouragement, kindness, and love you have shown me throughout the years. Stay PAWsome!

OUR TOMORROW

OTHER BOOKS FROM OUR TOMORROW

A BOOK SERIES WRITTEN BY YOUNG COMMUNITY LEADERS AND ACTIVISTS, DEDICATED TO INSPIRING, UPLIFTING, AND EMPOWERING THE NEXT GENERATION OF LEADERS

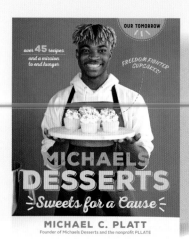

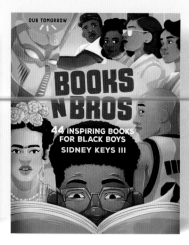

Michaels Desserts
Sweets for a Cause
Michael Platt

A fun cookbook for all ages by teen baker, social entrepreneur, and food justice advocate Michael C. Platt, inspired by his mission to end food insecurity one dessert at a time. Recipes include No Kid Hungry French Toast Breakfast Cupcakes, Nelson Mandela Malva Pudding Cupcakes, and Booker T. Washington Vegan Chocolate Cupcakes.

ISBN 9781684620470

Books N Bros
44 Inspiring Books for Black Boys
Sidney Keys III

From teen entrepreneur and literacy advocate Sidney Keys III, a reading guide that centers on Black boys, inspired by the success of his book club Books N Bros. Featured books include *Hidden Figures: Young Readers' Edition* by Margot Lee Shetterly, *Black Boy White School* by Brian F. Walker, and *Shuri: A Black Panther Novel* by Nic Stone.

ISBN 9781684620487

Kindness Is My Hobby
How to Change the World Right Where You Are
Ruby Kate Chitsey

Ruby Kate Chitsey, the teenage founder and CEO of Three Wishes for Ruby's Residents, shares how she spreads kindness every day and how you can do it too, with activities inspired by her own initiatives that have gained her national attention. Projects include Senior Pen Pal Project, Mobile Book Cart, and Postcards of Kindness.

ISBN 9781684620609